Family Violence: Beyond the Bruises

by

Nicole A. Maiocco
and
Mike Maiocco

Family Violence: Beyond the Bruises

by

Nicole A. Maiocco and Mike Maiocco

Published by
Police and Fire Publishing
1800 N. Bristol #C408
Santa Ana, CA 92707

Visit our website at: www.hiredbypolice.com

Cover design by
Michael Jo

Printed in the United States of America
June 2009

ISBN 978-0-9821157-8-7

QR (Quick Response) codes

http://www.westwood.edu

QR (Quick Response) codes incorporate advanced technology to deliver a reality-based application beyond the textbook. The subject matter "comes to life" through a video clip, complete with the sights and sounds unique to each chapter; each QR code offers a broader perspective of the material being taught and a better understanding of how it is applied in the field.

QR codes can be quickly accessed with a cell phone and are tailor-made for quick and easy linking to content on smart phones. Simply point the phone's camera at the QR code you wish to scan. There are a number of apps in the iPhone App Store that can read QR codes, including the free QR Reader. Most Android phones and Blackberries read the codes right out of the box, as can newer Nokia headsets. For older Androids and Blackberries, download free QR reader applications. Windows Mobile users can download Quick Marks.

This amazing technology is available to everyone, even if you do not own a smart phone. Visit http://www.pfpqrcodes.com in your web browser and access all QR codes pertaining to Police and Fire Publishing books by simply clicking on the book title. Utilizing supplemental media has never been easier!

Dedication

This book is dedicated to the two most important people in my life: my husband Mike and our son, AJ. I wouldn't be the person I am today without both of you. You make me a stronger, kinder and more grateful woman. Thank you for always supporting me, encouraging me and loving me unconditionally. I am honored to be your wife and mother! To my husband and co-author, thank you for encouraging me to do something I never thought I could do and for all your help along the way!

And to the thousands of survivors of family violence out there living life courageously each and every day; you are an inspiration to many. For those survivors who haven't yet found the courage to leave an abusive situation, take heart and know that you can do it. There are people who want to help. You are stronger and more courageous than you think you are!

Note from the Publisher, Pete Bollinger

As a police officer who started in the 1980's, I can tell you firsthand how we "handled", or more truthfully "didn't handle", family violence calls. Actions we would take at a family violence call included tactics that would get an officer fired today:

- Drive the suspect to a relative's house giving him an opportunity to "cool down"
- Advise him to send flowers the next day
- Encourage the couple to hug and "end the problem"
- Hit the suspect so he "knows what it feels like"
- Tell her she should have dinner ready on time for her husband
- Tell her she doesn't work so she should have a clean house

As one officer stated, "Twenty years ago, police work was different. We were there to solve the problem and that's what we did. Only now I realize we not only minimized the victim, we unwittingly helped perpetuate the cycle of violence." Officers today have a much better understanding of family violence and work with, not against, all types of social services.

Table of Contents

Introduction

Family violence crimes are the most committed, least reported crimes in the United States. They are also the underlying cause of most crimes that are committed in America. This book will address those topics that are most commonly faced in order to give the reader an overview and basic understanding of family violence. Family violence is widely misunderstood; people wonder why the victim doesn't just leave or believe it only happens in low-income families, only the victim and her abuser are affected so it should just remain a private matter. The list of misconceptions goes on and on.

Rather than calling them victims, the proper term for women waging the battle of family violence should be "survivor". A survivor is "a person who continues to function in spite of opposition, hardship, or setbacks". After working closely with victims of family violence for many years, attending hundreds of hours of training, and working alongside District Attorneys, Judges and police officers, I have been a firsthand observer to things I never thought I would see in my lifetime. I have walked with survivors through some of the darkest days of their lives. I have been a first responder, alongside police officers, on thousands of calls to provide crisis intervention to the families involved. These survivors are some of the strongest, most resilient people I have ever met. Most of them are doing everything they can to protect themselves and their children. They live every day in fear, yet they still believe in their families and are holding on to hope for a different future.

Family violence is a difficult and complex issue. It truly is an insidious evil that has woven itself into the fabric of our society. And while I don't claim to have all the answers, I do hope this book will provide some insight on the various pieces in play when dealing with family violence. As more and more people become educated on this issue, I do believe that we can dramatically change the direction and future for thousands of victim's lives.

Warning: The following clip contains a very emotional subject involving a child

http://www.youtube.com/watch?v=oMZkQvAsedg

http://www.youtube.com/watch?v=ANqGB0xG8-w

Author's notes:

- While it is understood that both men and women can be (and are) victims of family violence, national statistics indicate that approximately 85% of victims are women. From a professional and personal standpoint, out of thousands of cases, I have assisted a handful of male victims. There are no doubt more male victims than those that report it, but for societal reasons (e.g. embarrassment), men rarely report abuse. For this reason and for ease of reading, this book will refer to victims as women and abusers as men.

- Every story told in this book is true. They are stories of people I have encountered and spent time with during my career. All names have been changed to protect the innocent.

Chapter 1: Dynamics of Family Violence

Family violence has increased at alarming rates over the past several years. Every year, family violence is the number one cause of injury to women ages 18-45, requiring more medical attention than rape, car accidents and muggings combined. In fact, every 9 seconds, a woman in the United States is battered and every day three women are murdered.

What is Family Violence?

http://www.youtube.com/watch?v=mvpZzNxXOJw

So what exactly is family violence? According to *wikipedia.org*, family violence "occurs when a family member, partner or ex-partner attempts to physically or psychologically dominate another". It can occur between couples who are married, living together or dating, gay or straight, young or old. Family violence doesn't discriminate and is one of the few crimes that cross all lines of age, race, culture, ethnicity, economics, socioeconomics, gender and religion. Both men and women can be either the victim or the perpetrator.

There are four types of violence that are most commonly referred to when addressing family violence:

- verbal/emotional abuse

- financial abuse

- physical abuse

- sexual abuse

Although verbal/emotional and economic abuse is not necessarily against the law, they are definitely precursors to more aggravated forms of abuse as we will discuss in more detail later in this chapter.

http://www.youtube.com/watch?v=VWTAdfIc4kQ

Verbal/Emotional Abuse

Statistics show that in most instances, before any physical abuse takes place, there is a long history of verbal and/or emotional abuse. This type of abuse starts slowly and eventually wears down the victim's self-esteem. It can include constant criticism, making humiliating remarks (especially in public places), not responding to what the victim says, mocking, name-calling, yelling, swearing, interrupting, etc. It could be something as small as giving the victim an intimidating look or something as obvious as isolating her from her family and friends. Victims begin to believe the things their abuser is telling them because they are hearing them day after day and as the isolation begins, the victim has less people telling her something different.

Financial Abuse

This includes not paying bills, refusing to give the victim money, not letting the victim work outside the home, interfering with the victim's job, refusing to work and support the family, etc. While none of this is against the law, they are certainly ways for the abuser to gain control over the victim and to continue to place her in a powerless state.

Physical Abuse

Physical abuse is the most understood form of family violence. It includes hitting, slapping, kicking, choking, strangling, pushing, punching, etc. (There is a difference between choking and strangling although most people don't realize it. Choking is an internal event – choking on a piece of food or on something shoved down the throat; strangling is an external event – putting one's hands around the neck, etc.) Bruises, welts, red marks, and broken bones are among the injuries commonly incurred from physical abuse.

In the following pictures, the victim sustained significant bruising when her husband kicked her with his steel-toed work boots for "talking back" to him. After kicking her repeatedly in the buttocks and thigh area, he dragged her across the floor and shoved her up against the wall. These injuries are unfortunately not all that uncommon. The photographs were utilized as evidence to convict the abuser.

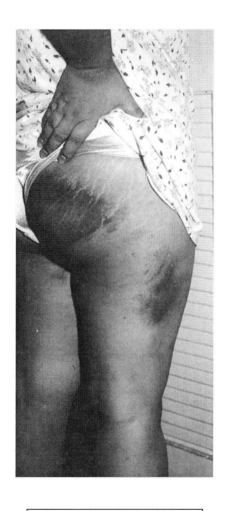

Dark purple and greenish bruises with a yellow and pink center on the victim's right buttock and outer right thigh

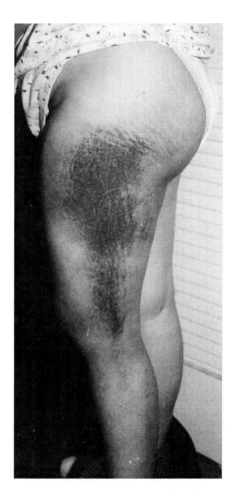

Dark purple bruises with red scrape marks on the victim's outer left thigh that run from the hip to the knee

Sexual Abuse

Sexual abuse includes forcing sex on an unwilling partner, demanding sexual acts that the victim does not want to perform or degrading treatment. Many victims don't realize they are being sexually abused. While this may sound strange to some people, to a woman who is being told she is "fat", "ugly" or "unwanted" on a regular basis, she easily sees sex as a way to pacify her abuser's anger. Victims are willing to do almost anything to abate the anger.

Date rape accounts for 67 percent of sexual assaults among teens and spousal rape accounts for 10 percent of all sexual assault cases. While hard to prove and even harder to prosecute, until recently, spousal rape was not even considered a crime in most states: it was believed that a husband could not rape his wife. After the feminist movement of the 1970s, laws began to change and spousal rape became a crime in all 50 states.

Although the specific definition of spousal rape varies from state to state, it is generally defined as any unwanted intercourse or penetration obtained by force or threat of force. While spousal rape can be a very gray area, it is important to understand that even if someone is married, no still means no. A woman has a right to say that she doesn't want to have sex. Rape isn't about love or passion or intimacy, it is about control.

Men who rape their partners are the most egocentric of all abusers. They want what they want when they want it. They believe their needs and wants are the most important thing in the world and they will do anything to satisfy them.

There are many different ways a man can rape his partner. For example, if she is tired or sick, he may wait until she is asleep before taking what he believes to be his to take; or he may get her so drunk that she passes out or is unable to say no. Spousal rape is extremely destructive to the victim. Sometimes it is physically damaging, but more often it is psychologically damaging as it is rarely a one time occurrence. This is a crime that isn't reported very often because most people don't understand that it is against the law for someone to force themselves on a spouse. Also, as with all types of sexual assault, the victim feels very ashamed that it happened and wonders if other people will believe her when she tells them about the abuse.

Cycle of Violence

The cycle of violence, or cycle of abuse, is the cycle that is typical of an abusive relationship. It contains four phases:

- **tension building phase**
- **acute violence phase**
- **honeymoon phase**
- **denial**

Every abusive relationship will run its course through this cycle although each phase can vary in length from couple to couple and even from incident to incident. On the next page is a pictorial representation of the cycle of violence followed by a detailed description of each phase.

http://www.youtube.com/watch?v=f__DFogTAqI

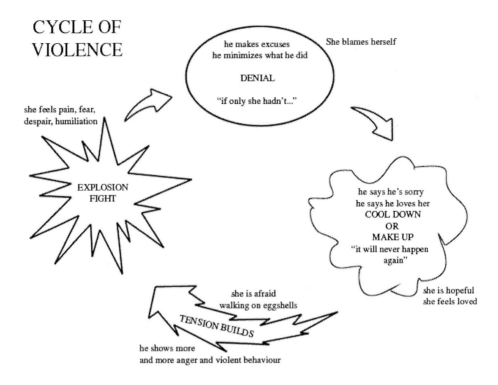

CYCLE OF VIOLENCE

he makes excuses
he minimizes what he did

DENIAL

"if only she hadn't..."

She blames herself

she feels pain, fear,
despair, humiliation

EXPLOSION
FIGHT

he says he's sorry
he says he loves her
COOL DOWN
OR
MAKE UP
"it will never happen
again"

she is hopeful
she feels loved

she is afraid
walking on eggshells

TENSION BUILDS

he shows more
and more anger and violent behaviour

Cycle of Violence

Developed by Our Lady of Good Counsel Society / Vancouver, Canada

Tension Building Phase

The tension building phase often includes verbal and/or emotional abuse. The victim is walking on eggshells. She is often aware that something is wrong, even though she may not know exactly what it is. The victim will typically try to stay out of her partner's way and/or work very hard to control the environment. For example, she will make sure dinner is ready on time, the kids are quiet, and the house is picked up. She will try to do anything and everything she can to avoid "setting him off". The challenge is that she usually does not know what action or reaction will set him off (and it likely changes from day to day). She lives in a constant state of anxiety waiting for the next incident. This phase could also include minor battering instances such as forcefully grabbing or holding her arm.

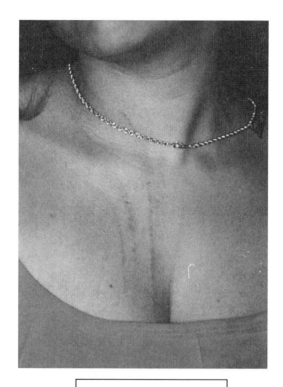

Vertical scratches
on the
victim's neck

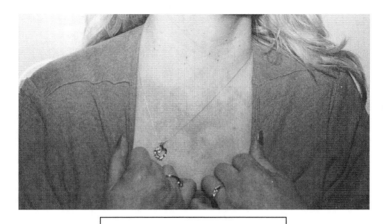

Redness on victim's neck
and chest from being
strangled

Acute Violence Phase

The acute violence phase is the second phase of the cycle. Terror and fear are established as physical violence begins to take place. The abuser will often have what is described as "out of control" anger. He is set-off by seemingly small things (which explain why the victim is trying so hard to control her environment) and has very unpredictable behavior. Severe emotional and physical damage can take place during this phase. Many victims say they are willing to take the abuse if it protects their children from being victims as well. What these victims don't realize is that a child simply witnessing abuse is considered to be a punishable offense on its own merit in many states and psychologically damaging in the long-term.

Honeymoon Phase

The next phase is the honeymoon phase. After the incident(s) of violence, the abuser is typically remorseful and sorry for what happened. There is always a reason or explanation for the behavior. The abuser will beg for forgiveness, say it was the last time, and often promise to go to counseling or get help. He says he will change and likely becomes loving and kind towards the victim. Over and over again, victims have reported that this phase is the reason they stay in the relationship. Victims truly care about their abuser or they wouldn't be in the relationship to begin with. They want to think the best of their partner and want to believe they are capable of changing. Often, the victims believe they are the only one who can help their partner change...and so they stay.

Denial Phase

The final phase is denial: denial for both the abuser and the victim. Here are some examples of denial:

> (1) The abuser may say the victim "deserved" the abuse (she just made him "so mad", she didn't have dinner ready on time, etc.). At the same time, the victim feels responsible and may also believe she deserved the abuse.

(2) The abuser may say, "I wasn't aware that I hit her so hard" or some other form of being "unaware". The abuser uses excuses like these which then allow the victim to give the abuser an "out" for his behavior, thus minimizing the situation.

(3) The abuser may believe he has the right to discipline the victim while the victim feels responsible to protect the relationship (thus enduring the abuse).

(4) The abuser may say the victim provoked his anger while the victim says, "that's just how he is". In all of these situations, both the victim and the abuser are minimizing the seriousness and severity of what is happening in their relationship.

Family violence is a learned behavior. Children learn it from their parents and when they are grown, they often bring it into their own relationships becoming either victims or abusers. Victims don't say, "I'm going to find an abusive relationship and live happily ever after." And abusers don't say, "I'm going to get in a relationship with someone I can beat up" Grasping this concept is one of the most important steps in understanding the cycle of violence. Knowledge that abuse is a learned behavior will affect how you approach the situation and how you deal with both the victim and the abuser. By the time the relationship becomes physically abusive, there is usually a long history between the couple. There are highly-charged emotions and feelings involved making these crimes unlike any other. In fact, family violence calls for service are the most dangerous calls that police officers respond to.

One Saturday afternoon in a mobile home park, a police department received a call of shots fired. Joanne, a young woman in her late teens, was living in a mobile home with her grandparents when her ex-boyfriend, Carl, showed up at the door. After a brief argument, Carl pulled out a semi-automatic pistol. Joanne ran inside the mobile home with Carl chasing her. Her grandfather tried to intervene and Carl shot him for his efforts, killing him almost instantly. Carl then pursued Joanne into her bedroom, dragged her outside to the front patio, put the gun against her chest and pulled the trigger. The bullet pierced her heart and killed her instantly. Carl then took the gun, placed it against his head and pulled the trigger; ending his own life as well. A records check was conducted on the serial number of the handgun and it was registered to a police officer in another county. An investigation revealed that Carl was the son of a police officer from the adjacent county. He had taken his father's service weapon as the father slept after working a graveyard shift. A note was found on the patio where both Carl and Joanne fell. The note stated "If I can't have you, no one will".

GROUP ACTIVITY

Break into small groups of 3-4 people. Read the following scenario and respond as if you were a police officer.

You receive a call to respond to a home for domestic violence. When you get there, Elva is crying hysterically. She tells you that she and her boyfriend, Jose, were lying in bed when they started arguing. According to Elva, Jose thought she wanted to have sex, but she didn't. When she tried to tell him she didn't want to have sex, he started yelling at her, calling her a "stupid whore". She said Jose got up on his knees and hit her approximately 8 times on her buttocks and legs. Elva said she covered her face, started to cry, got up and went to the bathroom to try to calm down. She came back into the bedroom, got dressed, and went into the living room to call 911. Elva said she didn't have a chance to talk to the dispatcher because Jose followed her and as soon as he saw she was calling the police, he pulled the phone out of her hands. She said he pulled it out of her hands so hard, that he ripped the phone and wires from the wall. She said Jose then tried to pull her back into the bedroom putting his hand over her mouth as he continued to tell her to "shut up". Elva says she was screaming and crying when Jose's cousin and his girlfriend came into the apartment. When Jose saw the couple, he got off of Elva where he had her pinned on the floor. Jose tells you that nothing happened. Elva was just overreacting to a minor argument. The cousin and girlfriend have left and Jose says he isn't sure where they went. Elva asks that you arrest him and take him away.

Questions:
   (1) Identify victim(s) and suspect.
   (2) Identify potential injuries.
   (3) Identify and list crime violations.
   (4) Outline your course of action.

25

Power and Control

Power and control are at the root of family violence. Physical and even sexual abuse is never the reason someone is abused; rather it is the result of one person attempting to gain control over another. Abusers seek to gain and then maintain control over their victims using a variety of methods. The power and control wheel illustrated on the following page is used to understand the overall pattern of abusive and violent behaviors. Below is a thorough description of each section of the wheel.

 http://www.youtube.com/watch?v=qvm8E-zg_RU

Using Intimidation

Intimidation is all about fear – both real and perceived. Abusers will often do anything they can to instill a sense of fear in their victims; fear the abuser will then use to coerce the victim to behave in any manner the abuser wants, or fear the abuser will use to force the victim to stay in the relationship even after the victim wants to leave. Once she is afraid, she is less able to do anything about the situation. Punching walls, destroying furniture, throwing things, breaking dishes, and destroying or damaging personal belongings of the victim are all ways for an abuser to cause his victim to fear him. These behaviors are seen when a victim tries to leave her abuser or after the couple has broken up. Intimidation is a very real form of emotional violence. The abuser may follow or stalk his victim oftentimes at her place of employment.

Power and Control Wheel

Developed by Domestic Abuse Intervention Project / Duluth, MN

http://www.youtube.com/watch?v=7v2LmM_FO-U

He may embarrass the victim in public, yelling at her or putting her down. He may constantly check up on her, insisting that she answer her cell phone every time he calls. Or he may refuse to leave when she asks him to. Harassment of this nature is often the basis for restraining orders granted by the court to protect the victim from her abuser.

Using Emotional Abuse

Emotional abuse is where family violence typically begins – the foundational building block for ongoing and future abuse. Emotional abuse can be very subtle and a victim may not realize it is happening until it has been going on for quite some time. The abuser will create an environment in which the victim feels bad about herself and thus, lowering her self-esteem. He will call her names and convince her that no one else would want to be with her because she is so ugly, fat, lazy, etc. Abusers also often play manipulative mind games making the victim feel like something is wrong with her rather than the abuser. For example, he may treat her terribly, call her names, humiliate her, make her feel guilty about going out with friends or any number of things. However, if he only does those things to her when they are alone and in public he is charming, kind, sweet, and dynamic, he can try to convince her that she is the problem. And oftentimes, because everyone else (besides the victim) has such wonderful things to say about him, she may start to believe that she is exaggerating the situation or too hard on herself.

Using Isolation

Domestic violence is typically a very private matter, most often happening behind closed doors. It isn't something that people like to talk about and it certainly isn't something anyone wants to admit is happening to them. The embarrassment of the situation and her belief that nobody would understand her position initially cause the victim to become very isolated. This makes it even easier for the abuser to use isolation as a means of control. He can make it hard for her to see friends and family, monitor her phone calls, mail and computer activity – or limit access to them all together. He can control where she goes, what she does, and what she has, even within her own home. He can take her car keys away or keep her from learning how to drive. He can limit her access to money and/or limit her knowledge of the family's financial situation.

Minimizing, Denying, Blaming

An abuser will use any and all means possible to deny the reality of abuse. He may make light of the abuse that is happening saying things like, "Don't be such a wimp – I didn't hit you *that* hard!" or "I was just playing around – why do you have to take everything so seriously?" Or he may shift responsibility for his abusive behavior making her believe she caused it: "If you would just have dinner ready when I come home from work, then I wouldn't have to yell at you."

Using Children

An abuser will use his children as a means to gain power and control over his victim by making threats. He may threaten to take the children away from her, threaten physical harm to the children, or threaten to tell the children what the victim is "really like". Because moms have a natural instinct to protect their children, victims will usually go to any lengths to protect them from the abuser. And because abusers know this about their victims, this becomes a very effective form of control for them to use.

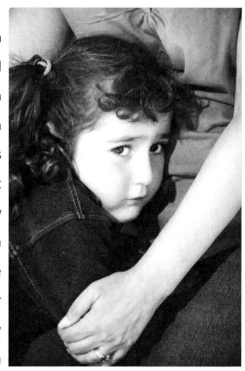

Matt was angry with his wife Lonnie and they got into an argument. Matt grabbed their one year old son and ran into the garage. Lonnie called the police and then went to look for Matt. She walked into the garage just as

Matt was sprinkling gas on and around him and their baby. He then opened the valve to his barbeque grill which released gas with a hissing sound. When the officers arrived, they tried to diffuse the situation, but when they stepped closer to Matt, he pulled out a lighter, showing them he was ready to strike the marker with his thumb. After they had all been standing in the fumes for close to an hour, everyone's mental abilities were being impacted, creating temple-pounding headaches. After an extended negotiation, the child was released and a few minutes later, Matt submitted to arrest. When the case went to court, Lonnie minimized the event and Matt only served 90 days in jail. About a year later, the same officers were dispatched to the same residence: Lonnie and Matt having another argument. This incident did not rise to a criminal level and they were both counseled without further action. One of the officers asked Lonnie why she lied in court. She said, "If Matt is in jail, he can't work. How are we going to survive?"

Using Male Privilege

Lying, breaking promises, withholding important information, being unfaithful, being overly jealous and hoarding money are all ways for a man to act like the master of the house. He makes one set of rules for him and another set for his partner. He may define male and female roles within the household, treating his partner more like a servant than a partner. Abusers may also make a point of making all the big decisions for the family without consulting his partner; thus showing her who is really in charge in their relationship. Ultimately she is left feeling like it is not a relationship of equality and that she doesn't have a voice in their family. And in truth, she doesn't.

Using Financial Abuse

In today's society, it is typical for both the male and female to work outside of the home. However, in abusive relationships, the abuser may prevent his partner from getting a job. He may present it in a way that is flattering – "Babe, I don't want you to have to work outside of our home" – who wouldn't want to hear that? But what an abuser really means is – "Babe, I want you to stay home so I know exactly who you are talking to and where you are every minute of the day". If he is the only wage earner, it is also easier for him to give her an "allowance" or limit her access to money (i.e. put all the bank accounts in his name).

One case I worked in a very affluent area was a great example of financial abuse. Someone had called the police when they heard the neighbors, Jack and his wife Marie, arguing and what sounded like things breaking. After being arrested for domestic violence, Jack was being arraigned in court. Marie came to his arraignment and asked to speak with the judge. This wasn't all that uncommon as victims often ask to speak to the judge on behalf of their partner (usually to ask for his immediate release).

However, Marie's case was a bit different. She wasn't denying that the abuse had taken place, she simply wanted the judge to release her husband because she had no money. Although they were very wealthy and lived in a huge house, Jack maintained all access to the family finances and Marie didn't even have enough money to buy herself lunch without "permission"! With her husband in jail, she was on the verge of being homeless. She had no means to pay their bills, put gas in her car or even buy groceries.

Using Coercion and Threats

The abuser will often make the victim feel guilty; that she is to blame for everything that goes wrong, whether or not she was involved in the situation. He will push the victim into making decisions, manipulate their children or other family members, insist on always being right or even make up impossible "rules" for the victim to follow and then punish her for breaking them.

Oftentimes a threat alone is enough for the victim to remain with her abuser. If harm is threatened to her children, her family or even their pets, a victim will stay in the relationship to protect others around her. He may tell her that if she calls the police the children will be taken away or if she is an illegal immigrant, she may be told that she will be deported if she reports the abuse.

Abusers will also use their physical size to intimidate the victims – the victim knowing he is much stronger and capable of seriously injuring her. Keeping weapons in the home and threatening to use them is another typical threat. Sometimes abusers will threaten, or even attempt, to harm themselves in an effort to prevent the victim from leaving. He will abuse drugs or alcohol, threaten self-harm or suicide, drive recklessly or deliberately do things that will cause trouble. It isn't uncommon for victims to report that their partner said he would kill himself if she left. Victims often feel like they are the only ones who can help the abuser "get better".

Of course there are potentially hundreds of ways for one person to exert power and control over another. And the better someone knows their partner, the better they will be able to wield that power and control using exactly what will work on that particular person. For example, one victim with whom I worked, Jane, absolutely adored her grandmother. She was the only person in Jane's family that had really cared about her and for her during Jane's most formative years. When Jane's relationship with her boyfriend became physically abusive, all her boyfriend had to do was remind her that he knew where he grandmother lived to keep her quiet about the abuse. Jane knew what her boyfriend was capable of doing to her and she just couldn't risk finding out what he might do to her grandmother. While this was a very effective way to control Jane, it is quite possibly a threat that wouldn't work on someone else.

In addition, it is important to note that while some of these forms of power and control are arrestable offenses, others alone may not be. However, they are all signs of domestic violence and what many professionals in the field call "red flags". A "red flag" is a warning sign of something more serious to come. Intimidation, minimizing, blaming, and name calling are not elements of a healthy, thriving relationship. They should instead be warning signs that something is wrong. In a relationship, it may be that two people are simply stressed out or overwhelmed with the demands of life; these may be signs that it is time to get help, often in the form of counseling or therapy. But when one or both partners aren't willing to get help for harmful behaviors or there seems to be an escalation of violence, it is clearly more than two people just having a bad day.

Why Women Stay

1.    2.

1. http://www.youtube.com/watch?v=-jw-QNwhFwE
2. http://www.youtube.com/watch?v=W_Hh-LJsya4

There are as many reasons why women stay, as there are women who stay! Every person is unique, and every abusive relationship is unique. Who the victim is, who the abuser is, each person's life history, experiences and beliefs, all add up to create a very unique situation. Even so, there are several common reasons why women stay in abusive relationships:

(1) *Frequency and severity*

Generally speaking the less severe and less frequent the incident, the more likely it is that a woman will stay. It's also possible that battering may occur over a very short period of time. Sometimes this may convince a woman to stay if the good times outnumber the bad. An abuser will also tell his victim that this was the last time. And because she wants to believe the best of her partner, she'll be convinced.

(2) *Her childhood*

If a victim grew up in a home where her father beat her mother, she will be more likely to accept abuse as a natural part of any relationship. To someone who hasn't been exposed to an abusive relationship, this might sound crazy. But keep in mind that abuse takes place behind closed doors and isn't something talked about. Therefore it makes it easier for someone to believe that abuse is natural.   In the same vein, the more a victim was abused (either physically or emotionally) by her own parents, the more likely she will stay in an abusive relationship.   Many, many times, if violence is present in the home, the children are being abused as well. This means she learned at an early age that it's okay to be violent with someone you love when they do something wrong. Another contributor from her childhood could be religion or cultural backgrounds.   Leaving may be offensive, embarrassing, or simply unacceptable to the family.   A person's religion may not accept leaving or may consider her to be a bad wife, mother, or person for doing so.

(3) *Economic dependency*

The victim may be economically dependent on her husband and see no real alternative to provide for her children.   Economic conditions today afford a woman with children few viable options.   If she has limited or no marketable skills, combined with the cost of childcare, it could seem impossible for a woman to believe she could make it on her own.   And while some government assistance is available, it is limited and many women dread the idea of using welfare.   Abusers also create their partner's dependency by controlling the family money and allowing her limited or no access to cash, checks, or other important documents.

(4) *Fear*

A victim believes her partner to be almost omnipotent. She sees no real way to protect herself from him. If she or someone else reports him to the police, he will likely take revenge on her, the children, her family members, and/or friends. Often an abused woman is so terrified she will deny abuse when questioned. Or she simply isn't willing or able to recognize it as abuse. Abusers instill a great amount of fear in their victims through their many attempts at gaining power and control, and with threats. Because so many things an abuser does creates this sense of fear for a victim, in truth, she has many valid reasons to be afraid.

(5) *Isolation*

Often an abuser has strategically arranged himself to be the victim's only support system having cut her off from other relationships with family and friends. Because abuse causes people to feel uncomfortable, they tend to withdraw from a relationship with a victim because of their uncertainty in dealing with the situation. Also, a victim may feel trapped, having no idea that thousands of services are readily available to her.

(6) *Low self esteem*

Learned helplessness often explains a battered woman's inability to act on her own behalf. She learns that her behavior has no effect on the outcome of a situation, since she is repeatedly abused with no logical consequences from preceding incidents. She believes what he says about her being incompetent and unable to function on her own. He is usually violent only with her and so she concludes that there must be something wrong with her. She then accepts his reasoning that she "deserved" the punishment or maybe he was just too drunk to know what he was doing. Some women believe that if they would improve or stop making mistakes, the battering would stop. They remain through guilt. Or quite simply, victims believe they have no power to change their situation.

(7) *Beliefs about marriage*

As mentioned earlier, a victim may believe that battering is a part of every marriage. Many women stay for the sake of their children needing a father. It sounds silly to someone who hasn't been in this situation, but time and time again, women have stayed thinking that a bad father is better than no father at all. Other beliefs about marriage include religious and cultural values which are imprinted from a young age. Many women are raised to believe in the importance of a good relationship with a man and the belief that relationships are a woman's responsibility to maintain.

(8) *Her beliefs about her husband*

Despite what is sometimes years of abuse, victims truly love their abuser and are emotionally dependent on them. Because victims believe their abusers to be all powerful, she believes her abuser will be able to find her anywhere she goes. Many of her fears and beliefs about him are based on reality, since some of the violence exhibited by these men is deadly. In addition, victims are often motivated by pity and compassion thinking they are the only one who can help the abuser overcome his problem.

http://www.youtube.com/watch?v=J7cumti-Pg8

Abuser Threat Assessment

Victims know their abuser better than anyone else. So when a victim gets to the point that she believes (or even just feels like) her abuser is going to kill her, it is important to take her seriously. Experts in the field agree that there are certain factors that can serve as statements of potential lethal violence in an abusive relationship. An explanation and examples of each are on the following pages.

(1) *Past violence*

Women who have been abused by their partner remain in a constant state of awareness, always anticipating the next act of violence. Frequency and escalation of violence can increase the risk of lethality. It can be helpful to note what previously triggered the most violent abuse and whether or not the current situation is similar.

(2) *Stated intention to kill*

Has the abuser made statements about wanting to kill himself or the victim? Is there a history of threats? Is there an escalation of the threats? Does the abuser have access to weapons? A positive answer to any of these questions indicates a greater risk of lethality.

(3) *Batterer's need to control / possess the victim*

As previously noted in the section on power and control, there are varying types and degrees of control that an abuser will use. Some abusers are more controlling than others using statements such as, "If I can't have you, nobody will" or "I can't live without you". Abusers who feel entitled to their partner's loyalty may have an underlying belief that their partner has no right to autonomy or a life without him. If a batterer feels threatened that the abuser is trying to leave, the situation could escalate. Stalking can also be seen as a sign of obsession and aggression.

(4) *Alcohol or drug use*

Being under the influence of alcohol or drugs seriously diminishes one's capacity. For many abusers, the violence escalates along with an increased use of alcohol or drugs. A past history of violence that accompanies alcohol or drug use should be taken into consideration – especially if there is a recent increase in alcohol or drug use.

(5) *Previous criminal history / normalization of violence*

Familiarity with violence may provide the abuser with the ability to normalize the abuse. It is important to look at any history of violence including abuse he may have suffered or witnessed as a child. A job that normalizes violence should also be assessed – police or correctional officers and military personnel are some examples. Prior arrests for violent offenses are also indicators of a heightened risk for future violence.

(6) *Emotional / mental functioning*

It is important to consider the mental and emotional state of the batterer including such things as depression, use of medication, seeing a therapist, or a history of any psychological disorders. His physical state should also be considered since a decline in overall health may indicate increased feelings of hopelessness or despair, leading to an increased potential for danger.

(7) *Isolation from others*

Many times the abuser not only tries to isolate the victim, but himself as well. If he has few support systems outside of the victim, his dependence on her naturally increases. Unfortunately, the danger to the victim also increases because he has nobody else to turn to.

(8) *Accessibility to victim*

If an abuser is threatening harm to the victim and she is easily accessible to him, there is an increased risk of harm to her. If a victim chooses to leave the relationship, but the abuser still knows where she is, people around her should know about the potential threat and work through a practical safety plan for everyone involved.

While this threat assessment can be a helpful tool for assessing a batterer's risk of lethality, family violence is a volatile issue and there are never any guarantees. The following story illustrates this perfectly.

Most Sunday mornings are pretty quiet for police officers unless there are calls for service left over from the night before. But on one particular Sunday, the calm, quiet morning was shattered with a call of multiple gunshots in a small, but busy shopping center. The police dispatcher said that a man was standing in the parking lot shooting at customers. Multiple police units responded and when the first unit was a block away, the police dispatcher said the shooter had reloaded his weapon and was continuing to shoot.

When the officer arrived, the shooter walked towards him holding the handgun. He then shocked the officer when he placed the gun on the roof of a car and raised his hands in the air; the officer quickly took him into custody. Paramedics were summoned for the only two people shot, a man and a woman, who later died at the hospital.

The subsequent investigation revealed that the woman, Maggie, was the estranged wife of the shooter, Jim. Jim and Maggie were going through a difficult divorce and Maggie's male companion on that day was her new boyfriend. The victims were getting a bite to eat at a restaurant located in the shopping center before heading for the airport to go on vacation. Jim followed Maggie and her boyfriend and then executed them in the parking lot. Interestingly, Jim was the owner of a small business in a nearby city. He was described as a very nice, average man who was friendly to everyone.

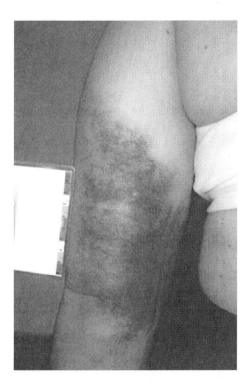

This victim got into an argument while driving in a car with her husband. When the argument escalated, she tried to get out of the vehicle. He reached over to keep her from leaving, and grabbed her by her sweater. He pulled her sweater so hard, it left an imprint on her arm. If you look closely at the photographs, you can see the waffle weave and seam of the sweater bruised into her arm.

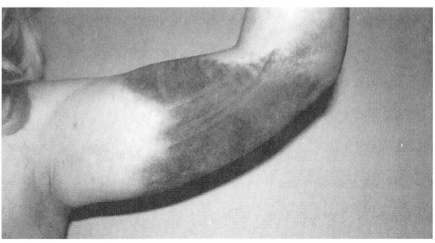

Personalized Safety Plans

http://www.youtube.com/watch?v=iufl_pUa4wE

Family violence victims are strongly encouraged to create a personalized safety plan. There are several variations of a plan: a plan for how to stay safe while in an abusive relationship, a plan of what to take once a decision is made to leave, and a plan of how to stay safe after leaving an abusive relationship.

(1) Staying safe in an abusive relationship

- During an explosive episode, try to avoid rooms without an exit (i.e. bathrooms) and rooms with weapons (i.e. kitchen)
- Practice how to get out of the house safely, identifying which windows and doors are usable
- Pack a bag with essential items that can be left in a secret, but accessible place
- Pick a code word to use with children, family and close friends so they know when the police need to be called
- Create a plan of where to go once the decision is made to leave the home (e.g. pick four places you could go that would be unknown to the abuser)

(2) What to take when leaving

- Children (if it is safe to do so)
- Money
- Keys to car, work, house
- Clothes
- Medication
- Important papers for you and your children
- Lease, rental agreement, house deed
- Birth certificates
- Social security cards
- School and medical records
- Credit cards and bank statements
- Driver's license
- Welfare identification
- Passports, green cards, work permits
- Insurance papers
- Protective Orders, divorce papers, custody papers
- Address book
- Pictures, jewelry, sentimental items
- Items for your children (e.g. clothes, small toy, comfort item)

(3) Staying safe after leaving an abusive relationship

- If you don't already have your own cell phone, get one

- If you don't have a restraining order, file for one

- If staying in the home, change the locks and consider installing stronger doors and an alarm

- Tell friends and neighbors the abuser no longer lives with you

- Tell the school or caregivers of your children who is authorized to pick up your children. If you have a restraining order, make sure the school or caregivers have a copy of it.

- Tell someone at work what has happened and make sure they also have a copy of the restraining order on file. If possible, have your calls screened.

- Avoid using the same stores and businesses you used when with your abuser.

Practical Learning Activity

You are victim of family violence and you need to create a personalized safety plan. Follow the guidelines outlined in this chapter to answer the questions below:

(1) Following the five suggestions for "staying safe in an abusive relationship", list how you would stay safe in your home.

(2) Create a detailed, specific list of what you would take with you if you had to leave your home in a hurry due to violence.

Regenerating Violent Family Cycle

Experts agree that a child who witnesses violence in the home is significantly more likely to be in an abusive relationship as an adult. In fact, according to Break the Cycle, an organization aiming to empower youth to end domestic violence, "witnessing violence between one's parents or caretakers is the strongest risk factor of transmitting violent behavior from one generation to the next." It is powerful and compelling to realize that violence is a learned behavior, it is not innate.

Male abusers believe women are inferior. He uses violence to obtain power at home. He is rigid and demanding, expecting obedience from his wife/girlfriend. He holds her responsible for his happiness and assumes a controlling position in all family matters. He does not see her as a partner, but rather someone that is subservient to him.

Female partners believe they are worthless and thus tolerate violence towards her. She assumes a passive role, feels helpless and relinquishes power to her mate. She accepts responsibility for the success of the marriage and for holding the family together.

Male children of family violence learn unhealthy and unrealistic expectations of marriage. He learns that men can control with violence and sees men as superior to women. He accepts minimal responsibility for his own behavior and learns that loved ones have the right to hurt one another.

Female children see the value of women as secondary to men. She accepts violence towards women as natural and a "normal" part of a marriage. She sees passivity as necessary for women. She feels that she will be unfulfilled unless she is married and a mother. She sees women as responsible for their mate's happiness and learns that loved ones have the right to hurt one another.

When you look at the various things that each person in the family is learning from the existing violence, it paints a clearer picture of why the violence continues. As crazy as it sounds to someone who has never been in an abusive relationship, violence becomes a normal part of life. Each person in the home is experiencing something very real, but all from very different perspectives. Unknowingly, children who grow up in abusive homes often seek out partners who shared the same experience, thereby creating yet another abusive relationship. Until one person (either the abuser or the victim) courageously decides to get help, the cycle of violence will continue.

Chapter Summary

- Family violence includes 4 types of violence:
  - Verbal/emotional abuse
  - Financial abuse
  - Physical abuse
  - Sexual abuse
- The cycle of violence is the cycle that is typical of an abusive relationship and contains four phases:
  - Tension building phase
  - Acute violence phase
  - Honeymoon phase
  - Denial
- Power and control are at the root of family violence and the power and control wheel is commonly used to understand this issue.
- There are as many reasons why women stay as there are women who stay. In spite of this, there are several common reasons why women stay in an abusive relationship:
  - Frequency and severity
  - Her childhood
  - Economic dependency
  - Fear

- Isolation
- Low self-esteem
- Beliefs about marriage
- Her beliefs about her husband

- An abuser threat assessment can be conducted to help assess the potential lethality of an abuser.

- Family violence victims are strongly encouraged to create a personalized safety plan which includes a place to stay in an emergency and a list of necessary items to quickly remove from the home.

- Experts agree that a child who witnesses violence in the home is significantly more likely to be in an abusive relationship as an adult.

http://www.youtube.com/watch?v=FjfZaswsbPs

Chapter Questions

(1) List the four types of violence and give an example of each.

(2) Describe the four phases of the cycle of violence.

(3) List three reasons women stay in abusive relationships and describe each.

(4) What is the abuser threat assessment and how is it used?

(5) What is the regenerating violent family cycle? Why is it important to understand?

Chapter 2: Family Violence Statistics

 http://www.youtube.com/watch?v=xYWxfxMOUO4

Myths about Family Violence

MYTH #1: Domestic violence does not affect many people.

- A woman is beaten every 15 seconds.

  (Bureau of Justice Statistics, Report to the nation on Crime and Justice, Oct 1983)

- Domestic violence is the leading cause of injury to women between ages 15 and 44 in the United States – more than car accidents, muggings, and rapes combined.

  (Uniform Crime Reports, Federal Bureau of Investigation, 1991)

- Battered women are more likely to suffer miscarriages and to give birth to babies with low birth weights.

  (Surgeon General, United States, 1992)

- Sixty-three percent of the young men between the ages of 11 and 20 who are serving time for homicide have killed their mother's abuser.

  (March of Dimes, 1992)

MYTH #2: Battering is only a momentary loss of temper.

- Battering is the establishment of control and fear in a relationship through violence and other forms of abuse. The batterer uses acts of violence and a series of behaviors, including intimidation, threats, psychological abuse, isolation, etc. to coerce and to control the other person. The violence may not happen often, but it remains as a hidden (and constant) terrorizing factor.
  (Uniform Crime Reports, Federal Bureau of Investigation, 1990)

- One in five women victimized by their spouses or ex-spouses report they had been victimized over and over again by the same person.
  (The Basics of Batterer Treatment, Common Purpose, Inc., Jamaica Plan, MA)

MYTH #3: Domestic violence only occurs in poor, urban areas.

- Women of all cultures, races, occupations, income levels, and ages are battered – by husbands, boyfriends, lovers and partners.
  (Surgeon General Antonia Novello, as quoted in Domestic Violence: Battered Women)

- Approximately one-third of the men counseled (for battering) are professional men who are well respected in their jobs and their communities, these have included doctors, psychologists, lawyers, ministers, and business executives.
  (For Shelter and Beyond, Massachusetts Coalition of Battered Women Service Groups, Boston< MA 1990)

MYTH #4: Domestic violence is just a push, slap or punch – it does not produce serious injuries.

- Battered women are often severely injured – 22 to 35 percent of women who visit medical emergency rooms are there for injuries related to ongoing partner abuse.

  (Boston Bar Journal, 33-4, July/August, 1989)

- One in four pregnant women has a history of partner violence.

  (Journal of the American Medical Association, 1992)

MYTH #5: It is easy for battered women to leave their abuser.

- Women who leave their batterers are at a 75% greater risk of being killed by the batterer than those who stay.

  (Barbara Hart, National Coalition Against Domestic Violence, 1988)

- Nationally, 50% of all homeless women and children are on the streets because of violence in the home.

  (U.S. Senate Committee on the Judiciary. Violence Against Women: Victims of the System, 1991)

- There are nearly three times as many animal shelters in the United States as there are shelters for battered women and their children.

  (Senate Judiciary Hearings, Violence Against Women Act, 1990)

Prevalence

General Facts

- One in four women (25%) has experienced domestic violence in her lifetime.

  (The Centers for Disease Control and Prevention and The National Institute of Justice, Extent, Nature, and Consequences of Intimate Partner Violence, July 2000)

- Estimates range from 960,000 incidents of violence against a current or former spouse, boyfriend, or girlfriend to 3 million women who are physically abused by their husband or boyfriend per year.

  (U.S. Department of Justice, Violence by Intimates: Analysis of Data on Crimes by Current or Former Spouses, Boyfriends, and Girlfriends, March 1998)

- Women accounted for 85% of the victims of intimate partner violence, men for approximately 15%.

  (Bureau of Justice Statistics Crime Data Brief, Intimate Partner Violence, 1993-2001, February 2003)

- Women ages 20-24 are at the greatest risk of nonfatal intimate partner violence.

  (Bureau of Justice Statistics, Intimate Partner Violence in the U.S. 1993-2004, 2006)

- Separated and divorced males and females are at a greater risk of nonfatal intimate partner violence.

(Bureau of Justice Statistics, Intimate Partner Violence in the U.S. 1993-2004, 2006)

- Women of all races are equally vulnerable to violence by an intimate partner.

(Bureau of Justice Statistics, Violence Against Women: Estimates from the Redesigned Survey, August 1995)

- Intimate partner violence affects people regardless of income. However, people with lower annual income (below $25K) are at a 3-times higher risk of intimate partner violence than people with higher annual income (over $50K).

(Bureau of Justice Statistics, Intimate Partner Violence in the U.S. 1993-2004, 2006)

- On average between 1993 and 2004, residents of urban areas experienced the highest level of nonfatal intimate partner violence. Residents in suburban and rural areas were equally likely to experience such violence, about 20% less than those in urban areas.

(Bureau of Justice Statistics, Intimate Partner Violence in the U.S. 1993-2004, 2006)

- Nearly 2.2 million people called a domestic violence crisis or hot line in 2004 to escape crisis situations, seek advice, or assist someone they thought might be a victim.

(National Network to End Domestic Violence)

- Studies show that access to shelter services leads to a 60-70% reduction in incidence and severity of re-assault during the 3 to 12 months follow up period compared to women who did not access shelter. Shelter services led to greater reduction in severe re-assault than did seeking court or law enforcement protection, or moving to a new location.

(Campbell, JC, PhD, RN, FAAN. Anna D. Wolf, Johns Hopkins University School of Nursing, Protective Action and Re-assault: Findings from the RAVE study.)

- Nearly three out of four (74%) of Americans personally know someone who is or has been a victim of domestic violence. 30% of Americans say they know a woman who has been physically abused by her husband or boyfriend in the past year.

  (Allstate Foundation National Poll on Domestic Violence, 2006. Lieberman Research Inc., Tracking Survey conducted for The Advertising Council and the Family Violence Prevention Fund, July – October 1996)

- Surveys in recent years indicate that about a quarter of the world's women are violently abused in their own homes. Community-based surveys have yielded higher figures – up to 50% in Thailand, 60% in Papua New Guinea and the Republic of Korea, and 80% in Pakistan and Chile. In the United States, domestic violence is the biggest single cause of injury to women, accounting for more hospital admissions than rapes, muggings, and vehicle accidents combined. Such figures suggest that assaults on women by their husbands or male partners are the world's most common form of violence.

  (UNICEF, State of the World's Children Report, 1995)

Domestic violence homicides

- On average, more than three women and one man are murdered by their intimate partners in this country every day. In 2000, 1,247 women were killed by an intimate partner. The same year, 440 men were killed by an intimate partner. Intimate partner homicides accounted for 30% of the murders of women and 5% percent of the murders of men.

  (Bureau of Justice Statistics Crime Data Brief, Intimate Partner Violence, 1993-2001, February 2003. Bureau of Justice Statistics, Intimate Partner Violence in the U.S. 1993-2004, 2006)

- Most intimate partner homicides occur between spouses, though boyfriends/girlfriends have committed about the same number of homicides in recent years.

  (Bureau of Justice Statistics, Intimate Partner Violence in the U.S. 1993-2004, 2006)

- The health-related costs of intimate partner violence exceed $5.8 billion each year. Of that amount, nearly $4.1 billion are for direct medical and mental health care services, and nearly $1.8 billion are for the indirect costs of lost productivity or wages.

  (Centers for Disease Control and Prevention, Costs of Intimate Partner Violence against Women in the United States, April 2003)

- About half of all female victims of intimate violence report an injury of some type, and about 20 percent of them seek medical assistance.

60

(National Crime Victimization Survey, 1992-96; Study of Injured Victims of Violence, 1994)

- Thirty-seven percent of women who sought treatment in emergency rooms for violence-related injuries in 1994 were injured by a current or former spouse, boyfriend or girlfriend. (U.S. Department of Justice, Violence Related Injuries Treated in Hospital Emergency Departments, 1997)

Dating violence

- Approximately one in five female high school students reports being physically and/or sexually abused by a dating partner. (Jay G. Silverman, PhD; Anita Raj, PhD; Lorelei A. Mucci, MPH; and Jeanne E. Hathaway, MD, MPH, "Dating Violence Against Adolescent Girls and Associated Substance Use, Unhealthy Weight Control, Sexual Risk Behavior, Pregnancy, and Suicidality," Journal of the American Medical Association, Vol. 286, No. 5, 2001)

- Forty percent of girls age 14 to 17 report knowing someone their age who has been hit or beaten by a boyfriend. (Children Now/Kaiser Permanente poll, December 1995)

Domestic violence and children

- In a national survey of American families, 50% of the men who frequently assaulted their wives also frequently abused their children. (Strauss, Murray A, Gelles, Richard J., and Smith, Christine. 1990. Physical

Violence in American Families; Risk Factors and Adaptations to Violence in 8,145 Families. New Brunswick: Transaction Publishers)

- On average between 1993 and 2004, children under age 12 were residents of households experiencing intimate partner violence in 43% of incidents involving female victims and 25% of incidents involving male victims.

(Bureau of Justice Statistics, Intimate Partner Violence in the U.S. 1993-2004, 2006)

- Studies suggest that 3.3 – 10 million children witness some form of domestic violence annually.

(Carlson, Bonnie E. (1984). Children's observations of interpersonal violence. Pp. 147-167 in A.R. Roberts (Ed.) Battered women and their families (pp. 147-167). NY: Springer. Straus, M.A. (1992). Children as witnesses to marital violence: A risk factor for lifelong problems among a nationally representative sample of American men and women. Report of the Twenty-Third Ross Roundtable. Columbus, OH: Ross Laboratories.)

Rape / sexual assault

- Three in four women (76%) who reported they had been raped and/or physically assaulted since age 18 said that an intimate partner (current or former husband, cohabiting partner, or date) committed the assault.

(U.S. Department of Justice, Prevalence, Incidence, and Consequences of Violence Against Women: Findings from the National Violence Against Women Survey, November 1998)

- One in five (21%) women reported she had been raped or physically or sexually assaulted in her lifetime.

  (The Commonwealth Fund, Health Concerns Across a Woman's Lifespan: 1998 Survey of Women's Health, 1999)

Stalking

- Annually in the United States, 503,485 women are stalked by an intimate partner.

  (Patricia Tjaden and Nancy Thoennes, Extent, Nature, and Consequences of Intimate Partner Violence, National Institute of Justice, 2000)

- One in 12 women and one in 45 men will be stalked in their lifetime, for an average duration of almost two years

  (Tjaden and Thoennes, "Stalking in America," Washington, DC: National Institute of Justice, U.S. Department of Justice, 1998)

- Seventy-eight percent of stalking victims are women. Women are significantly more likely than men (60 percent and 30 percent, respectively) to be stalked by intimate partners.

  (Center for Policy Research, Stalking in America, July 1997)

- Eighty percent of women who are stalked by former husbands are physically assaulted by that partner and 30 percent are sexually assaulted by that partner.

  (Center for Policy Research, Stalking in America, July 1997)

- Victims may experience psychological trauma, financial hardship, and even death.

(Mullen, Pathe, and Purcell, Stalkers and Their Victims, New York: Cambridge University Press, 2000)

- Seventy-six percent of female homicide victims were stalked prior to their death.

  (MacFarlane et al., "Stalking and Intimate Partner Femicide," Homicide Studies 3, no. 4 (1998): 300-16)

Medical

- In 1994, thirty-seven percent of all women who sought care in hospital emergency rooms for violence-related injuries were injured by a current or former spouse, boyfriend or girlfriend.

  (Rand, Michael R. 1997. *Violence-related Injuries Treated in Hospital Emergency Departments.* U.S. Department of Justice, Bureau of Justice Statistics. Washington, DC.)

- In 2000, 1,247 women, more than three a day, were killed by their intimate partners.

  (Rennison, Callie Marie and Sarah Welchans. 2003. *Intimate Partner Violence 1993-2001.* U.S. Department of Justice Bureau of Justice Statistics. Washington, DC. Retrieved January 9, 2004)

- In addition to injuries sustained during violent episodes, physical and psychological abuse are linked to a number of adverse physical health effects including arthritis, chronic neck or back pain, migraine and other frequent headaches, stammering, problems seeing, sexually transmitted infections, chronic pelvic pain, and stomach ulcers.

(Coker, A., Smith, P., Bethea, L., King, M., McKeown, R. 2000. "Physical Health Consequences of Physical and Psychological Intimate Partner Violence." *Archives of Family Medicine)*

Pregnancy

- Homicide is a leading cause of traumatic death for pregnant and postpartum women in the United States, accounting for 31 percent of maternal injury deaths. Evidence exists that a significant proportion of all female homicide victims are killed by their intimate partners.

(Chang, Jeani; Cynthia Berg; Linda Saltzman; and Joy Herndon. 2005. Homicide: A Leading Cause of Injury Deaths Among Pregnant and Postpartum Women in the United States, 1991-1999. *American Journal of Public Health*. 95(3):471-477; Frye, V. 2001. Examining Homicide's Contribution to Pregnancy-Associated Deaths. *The Journal of the American Medical Association*. 285(11))

- Each year, about 324,000 pregnant women in this country are battered by their intimate partners. That makes abuse more common for pregnant women than gestational diabetes or preeclampsia -- conditions for which pregnant women are routinely screened. However, few physicians screen pregnant patients for abuse.

(Gazmararian JA; et al. 2000. "Violence and Reproductive Health; Current Knowledge and Future Research Directions. "*Maternal and Child Health Journal*. 4(2):79-84; Parsons, L., et.al. "Violence Against Women and

Reproductive Health: Toward Defining a Role for Reproductive Health Care Services". *Maternal and Child Health Journal,* Vol. 4, No. 2, pg. 135. 2000.)

- Complications of pregnancy, including low weight gain, anemia, infections, and first and second trimester bleeding are significantly higher for abused women, as are maternal rates of depression, suicide attempts, tobacco, alcohol, and illicit drug use. (Parker, B., McFarlane, J., & Soeken, K. 1994. "Abuse During Pregnancy: Effects on Maternal Complications and Infant Birthweight in Adult and Teen Women." *Obstetrics & Gynecology.* 841: 323-328; McFarlane, J. Parker B., & Soeken, K. 1996. "Abuse during Pregnancy: Association with Maternal Health and Infant Birthweight." *Nursing Research.* 45: 32-37; McFarlane, J., Parker, B., & Soeken, K. 1996. "Physical Abuse, Smoking and Substance Abuse During Pregnancy: Prevalence, Interrelationships and Effects on Birthweight." *Journal of Obstetrical Gynecological and Neonatal Nursing.* 25: 313-320.)

Domestic Violence in the Workplace

For many women, the violence doesn't end at home. It is widely believed that victims of family violence are especially vulnerable in the workplace. Victims may be harassed at work by threatening phone calls, miss work because of injuries or have lowered productivity due to the stress of being in an abusive relationship. One victim I worked with had recently lost her job because her boyfriend repeatedly called her workplace. But it wasn't just a call here and a call there, he called so many times, and used multiple phones at once, that he crashed the company's phone system. The employer lost money and potential clients when nobody in the company could be reached on the phone. Rather than help the victim, and what he called "her" problem, he let the victim go so "it would be easier on everyone involved". What the employer failed to realize is that the abuser got exactly what he wanted: control over his victim.

Prevalence

- A study of domestic violence survivors found that 74 percent of employed battered women were harassed by their partner while they were at work.

  (Family Violence Prevention Fund. 1998. *The Workplace Guide for Employers, Unions and Advocates.* San Francisco, CA)

- Between 1993 and 1999 in the United States, an average of 1.7 million violent victimizations per year were committed against persons age twelve or over who were at work or on duty.

  (Duhart, Delis T. 2001. "National Crime Victimization Survey: Violence in the Workplace, 1993-1999." U.S. Department of Justice, Bureau of Justice Statistics. Washington, DC. Retrieved January 9, 2004 http://www.ojp.usdoj.gov/bjs/pub/pdf/vw99.pdf)

- Homicide was the second leading cause of death on the job for women in 2000.

  (*Census of Fatal Occupational Injuries: Table A-6 Fatal occupational injuries by worker characteristics and event or exposure, 2000.* U.S. Dept. of Labor, Bureau of Labor Statistics. Washington, DC. Retrieved January 9, 2004 http://www.bls.gov/iif/oshwc/cfoi/cftb137.txt)

- More than 29,000 acts of rape or sexual assault are perpetrated against women at work each year.

  (*Crime Characteristics: Summary Findings.* 2001. U.S. Dept. of Justice, Bureau of Justice Statistics. Washington, DC. Retrieved January 9, 2004. http://www.ojp.usdoj.gov/bjs/cvict_c.htm)

- More than 1 million women are stalked each year in the U.S., and over a quarter of them report missing work as a result of the stalking.

  (Tjaden, Patricia and Nancy Thoennes. 2000. *Extent, Nature and Consequences of Violence Against Women: Findings from the National Violence Against Women Survey.* The National Institute of Justice and the Centers for Disease Control and Prevention. Retrieved January 9, 2004. http://www.ncjrs.org/pdffiles1/nij/183781.pdf)

- Of the 4 million workplace crime incidents committed against females from 1993 through 1999, only 40 percent were reported to the police.

  (Duhart, Delis T. 2001. "National Crime Victimization Survey: Violence in the Workplace, 1993-1999." U.S. Department of Justice, Bureau of Justice Statistics. Washington, DC. Retrieved January 9, 2004 http://www.ojp.usdoj.gov/bjs/pub/pdf/vw99.pdf)

Employer's Perspectives

- Business leaders agree that domestic violence is a problem that affects their workplaces: 57 percent of senior corporate executives believe domestic violence is a major problem in society. One-third of them think this problem has a negative impact on their bottom line, and 40 percent said they were personally aware of employees and other individuals affected by domestic violence. Sixty-six percent believe their company's financial performance would benefit from addressing the issue of domestic violence among their employees.

(*Addressing Domestic Violence: A Corporate Response.* 1994. Roper Starch Worldwide. New York, NY)

Costs of Workplace and Domestic Violence

- The annual cost of lost productivity due to domestic violence is estimated at $727.8 million, with over 7.9 million paid workdays lost each year.

  (*Costs of Intimate Partner Violence Against Women in the United States.* 2003. Centers for Disease Control and Prevention, National Center for Injury Prevention and Control. Atlanta, GA. Retrieved January 9, 2004. http://www.cdc.gov/ncipc/pub-res/ipv_cost/IPVBook-Final-Feb18.pdf)

- In one case, a wrongful death action against an employer who failed to respond to an employee's risk of domestic violence on the job cost the employer $850,000.

  (Burke, D.F. January, 2000. "When Employees are Vulnerable, Employers are Too." *The National Law Journal.* Retrieved January 9, 2004. http://www.semmes.com/publications)

- The costs of intimate partner violence exceed $5.8 billion each year, $4.1 billion of which is for direct medical and mental health care services, much of which is paid for by the employer.

  (*Costs of Intimate Partner Violence Against Women in the United States.* 2003. Centers for Disease Control and Prevention, National Center for Injury Prevention and Control. Atlanta, GA. Retrieved January 9, 2004. http://www.cdc.gov/ncipc/pub-res/ipv_cost/IPVBook-Final-Feb18.pdf.)

- Employers are aware of this economic burden: 44 percent of executives surveyed say that domestic violence increases their health care costs.

  (*Addressing Domestic Violence: A Corporate Response.* 1994. Roper Starch Worldwide. New York, NY)

Many executives now believe that domestic violence is an issue worth addressing at the corporate level. According to a Fortune magazine interview of a group of CEOs, domestic violence affects the bottom line because it affects productivity. The CEOs believe it is a more dangerous and volatile issue than alcohol and/or drug addiction.

Employers can take action that can protect victims while they are at work. Organizations, no matter what type of workplace it is, can create policies to address issues of family violence. The Corporate Alliance to End Partner Violence is a "national nonprofit organization dedicated to reducing the costs and consequences of partner violence at work - and eliminating it altogether. From policies and programs to legal issues and legislation, CAEPV is a credible source for information, materials and advice". (www.caepv.org)

Practical Learning Activity

You are a high-level manager at a corporation and have been tasked with creating a policy for your organization that addresses family violence.

(1) Identify the corporation for whom you work. (Pick a recognizable and researchable company.)
(2) Visit www.caepv.org and find the links to the instructions for how to start a workplace program.
(3) Read through "Six Steps to Creating a Successful Workplace Program".
(4) Read "Creating a Partner Violence Workplace Policy".
(5) Using what you learned from reading the two documents, create a policy for your organization. Your policy should be thorough and complete, incorporating at least 7 of the 9 points listed in policy creation document.

Children

Experts estimate between 3.3 and 4.3 million children witness domestic violence in the home each year. Because this number is based on reported cases of abuse, it is believed that the actual number is much higher. If FBI and National Institute of Justice estimates of the prevalence of unreported domestic violence cases are accurate, the actual number could be as high as 25 million. This number is both staggering and sad.

Many states describe children who witness violence in the home as being victims of "second hand" abuse. This refers to children who are exposed to violence in the home, but aren't victims of physical abuse. The effects of witnessing abuse run the whole gamut: physical, psychological, developmental, emotional, social, verbal, and even psychosomatic.

Children interpret violence very differently from adults:

- Children believe it is all their fault — had they been "good" mom/dad wouldn't have gotten so angry with each other
- In abusive homes, children become "pseudo" adults, putting aside their own needs to care for the parent and younger siblings. They take over the task the parents have neglected
- Boys become overprotective of their mothers but later, as teens, they may become abusive of her
- Children begin to believe that the way to show love, and /or communicate with each other, is by pushing, shoving, hitting and saying mean things
- Children may identify with the aggressor because of their "apparent" strength

Child abuse is 15 times more likely to occur in homes where domestic violence is present. In addition, children raised in abusive homes learn to harm themselves. When they witness abuse on an ongoing basis, they begin to confuse violence with love. They also internalize the abuse, blaming themselves for the abuse and even abuse themselves by cutting (using a sharp object to cut their arms or legs) or using drugs and/or alcohol.

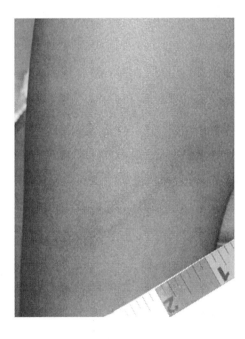

Welt on teenager's arm from dad slapping her when she tried to stop him from hitting her mom.

Children of violence witness extreme behavior. They don't learn positive ways to express their emotions. Witnessing substance abuse (drugs and/or alcohol) doesn't teach moderation or self-control. Also, children don't learn how to express anger or frustration without being cruel or abusive.

Children of violence do not learn boundaries. They constantly witness other people being violated. They have a hard time understanding and respecting physical and verbal boundaries. Boundaries are necessary, but there is a big difference between healthy ones and unhealthy ones. Children in abusive homes don't learn a difference, and they certainly don't learn how to establish *healthy* boundaries.

Children of violence take on adult roles prematurely. They become caretakers for their parents which can cause role-confusion for the child. Children are living in a tension filled environment and are forced to cope with "heavy" adult issues and problems. Children can easily become crutches for the parents to lean on and once this occurs, it is difficult to return to a "proper" parent/child relationship.

Violence results in stress, depression, and flashbacks for many children. For some, the depression is long-term and takes many years to recover from. Children may experience flashbacks or completely block out the violent incidents. Some even have severe and violent nightmares. In addition, repeated exposure to violence overwhelms and exhausts a child's nervous system.

Children of violence learn how to be violent toward others. Violence in the home teaches children how to treat others as objects rather than as people. Children learn specific techniques to hurt and humiliate others and that violence is the way to settle problems. Boys learn how to lash out at others and often become the school bully, are rebellious, turn to crime, or act out sexually. Girls learn how to accept and expect abuse and turn their anger inward or harm themselves. Children often become very angry with their mother for not protecting them.

An abusive home also means living in constant fear. It creates serious anxiety for children. They are forced to learn strategies of self-protection. They become watchful and jumpy, learning to read their parents' moves. Children never have the luxury of peace, even when they sleep – children are easily awakened by the violence or they sleep lightly in fear of danger. Violence also creates paranoia that every situation is a potentially dangerous one.

http://www.youtube.com/watch?v=_cZMhM9IW3c

http://www.youtube.com/watch?v=eh5fzzn_0NU

GROUP ACTIVITY

Break into small groups of 3-4 people. Read the following scenario and respond as if you were a police officer.

A 911 call comes in from an 11 year-old who reports that his father, Marcos, is drunk and hitting his mother, Alicia. At the house, Marcos answers the door and you smell a strong odor of alcohol. You see Alicia down the hall in the bedroom. She is visibly upset and crying. Her face is red and she has a scratch on the left side of her neck and shoulder. There is also a large bruise on her left arm. When you ask Alicia about her injuries, she says the bruise on her arm is from Marcos biting her several weeks ago when they were playing around. You see clear impressions of 2 bite marks on her arm. When asked what happened tonight, she continues to tell you that nothing is wrong. During your questioning, Alicia is constantly looking over at Marcos. She begs and pleads that her husband not be arrested because she is afraid of what he and/or his family will do to her. Alicia continues to refuse to tell you what happened tonight. She finally admits that the last time Marcos was arrested, her car tires were slashed and the interior of her home was vandalized. She tells you that Marcos controls all the money and the last time he was arrested, he refused to provide for her and their children. They have 4 children together, ages 13, 11, 10, and 5. When checking for wants or warrants on Marcos, you find 2 previous arrests: one for domestic violence and one for child abuse

Questions:
    (1) Identify victim(s) and suspect.
    (2) Identify potential injuries.
    (3) Identify and list crime violations.
    (4) Outline your course of action.

Chapter Summary

- There are several common myths about family violence:
    - It doesn't affect many people.
    - Battering is only a momentary loss of temper.
    - It only occurs in poor, urban areas.
    - It doesn't produce serious injuries.
    - It is easy for battered women to leave their abuser.
- Domestic violence is much more prevalent than most people realize – 25% of women will be victims of it in their lifetime.
- Victims of family violence are especially vulnerable in the workplace and many executives now believe that domestic violence is an issue worth addressing at the corporate level.
- Experts estimate between 3.3 and 4.3 million children witness domestic violence in the home each year. Because this number is based on reported cases of abuse, it is believed that the actual number could be as high as 25 million.
- Children of violence are impacted differently than adults:
    - They do not learn boundaries.
    - They take ob adult roles prematurely.
    - They experience stress, depression and flashbacks.
    - They learn how to be violent toward others.
    - They live in constant fear.

Chapter Questions

(1) List the three most troubling statistics you read in this chapter. Include the reason you found each one so powerful.

(2) What is the CAEPV? How do they help businesses?

(3) What is "second hand" abuse?

(4) What are two ways children interpret violence differently than adults?

(5) Why don't children who grow up in abusive homes learn healthy boundaries?

Chapter 3: Teen Dating Violence

Unique Characteristics

Teen dating violence is increasing at alarming rates. The most recent research revealed that 1 in 5 teens that have been in a serious dating relationship have been hit, slapped or pushed by their partner. Some people don't believe that this rate of violence is happening with teens, but it does happen and it is a very real problem.

Teen violence is in many ways similar to adult violence. The same cycle of violence and power and control wheel discussed earlier are applicable to teens and adults alike. The violence isn't about someone acting out after a bad day, but a repeated pattern of violent behavior. Just as adult violence will start with emotional or verbal abuse, so will teen violence. And just as adult violence will escalate to physical violence, so will teen violence.

Teens face intense pressure to be liked and accepted making their environment even more difficult for addressing violence. Peer pressure affects a teen's decision making, friend choices and so much more. Many teens feel pressured to be in a romantic relationship, even at a young age. And for teens that have an abusive home life, they are looking for an escape from the pain they are facing at home.

 http://www.youtube.com/watch?v=5bT4sGBpZiQ

Teen Power and Control

Power and control in teen relationships is very similar to power and control in adult relationships. The wheel illustrated on the following page is a helpful tool when talking to teens about a potentially abusive relationship and the various elements which can be addressed. Teens are smart, often much smarter than they are given credit for. Just as adult victims are aware they are in an abusive relationship, but don't see a way out, so are teens. Simply telling a teen to leave an abusive relationship can be harder than telling an adult. Even though a teen usually doesn't have children, a financial dependency or other reasons that adult women stay, they have many reasons of their own that can be equally as compelling. The second wheel is an equality wheel that illustrates the elements of a healthy teen dating relationship. Many parents and therapists like using the two side by side so the inequalities are highlighted even more so.

http://www.youtube.com/watch?v=KBih4C-zXYM

Peer Pressure
Threatening to expose someone's weakness or spread rumors • Telling malicious lies about an individual to peer group

Anger/Emotional Abuse
Putting him/her down • Making him/her feel badly about him or herself • Name calling • Making him/her think he/she's crazy • Playing mind games • Humiliating him/her • Making him/her feel guilty

Isolation/Exclusion
Controlling what another does, who he/she sees, and talks to, what he/she reads, where he/she goes • Limiting outside involvement • Using jealousy to justify actions

Using Social Status
Treating her like a servant • Making all the decisions • Acting like the "master of the castle" • Being the one to define men's and women's roles

Sexual Coercion
Manipulating or making threats to get sex • Getting her pregnant • Threatening to take the children away • Getting someone drunk or drugged to have sex

Intimidation
Making someone afraid by using looks, actions, gestures • Smashing things • Destroying property • Abusing pets • Displaying weapons

Threats
Making and/or carrying out threats to do something to hurt another • Threatening to leave, to commit suicide, to report him/her to the police • Making him/her drop charges • Making him/her do illegal things

Minimize/ Deny/Blame
Making light of the abuse and not taking concerns about it seriously • Saying the abuse didn't happen • Shifting responsibility for abusive behavior • Saying he/she caused it

Teen Power And Control Wheel

Physical • Violence • Sexual

Teen Power and Control Wheel

Adapted from the Domestic Abuse Intervention in Duluth, Minnesota

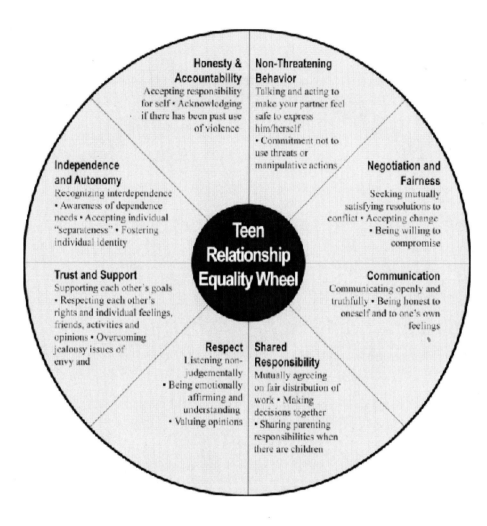

Teen Relationship Equality Wheel

Adapted from the Domestic Abuse Intervention in Duluth, Minnesota

GROUP ACTIVITY

Break into small groups of 3-4 people. Read the following scenario and respond as if you were a police officer.

You arrive at a park where both parties report violence. The calling party is 16 year old Denise who is at the park with Adam, her 18 year old boyfriend.

Denise says she came to the park with Adam to hang out. They were joking around and he playfully punched her on the arm. She did the same back to him. Out of nowhere, he "cold cocked" her across the face with his fist. She fell down and as she was laying there, he stood over her and told her to get up because he was just joking around. Adam tells you that he and Denise were just hanging out when she punched him on the arm so he punched her back. He says it was no big deal and that she is just a crazy nut that overreacts to everything.

When asked, Denise says that Adam didn't mean it. He is just stronger than he realizes. She tells you that a few days ago they were hugging, but it he started squeezing her tighter and tighter until she couldn't breathe. When she told him to stop, he said he was just being affectionate and most girls would kill to have a boyfriend like him. He also calls her names a lot, but she says she probably deserves it.

Denise has a red, swollen mark on her cheek and Adam has mild redness on his upper arm.

Questions:
  (1) Identify victim(s) and suspect.
  (2) Identify potential injuries.
  (3) Identify and list crime violations.
  (4) Outline your course of action.

Recognizing the signs

The dynamics of teen dating violence are slightly different from adults as teens have less experience and maturity in navigating through relationships. They are also seeking independence from their parents and can easily confuse abuse with love. There are several warning signs to be aware of that can help identify an abusive relationship:

(1) Constant Communication

In today's world of instant communication (e.g. cell phones, MySpace, Facebook, Twitter, instant messaging, text messaging, etc.), there are thousands of ways to stay in contact with one another. Unfortunately, this is also a way for an abuser to "keep watch" over his partner. Abusive partners can constantly call, text message, and use other means to keep tabs on their partner, wanting them to always be available or monitor their communication with friends. He may constantly demand to know where his partner is, what she is doing, who she is talking to, spending time with, etc. Or he may tell her he is going to call at 7p.m. and of course by 6:45p.m., she is waiting by the phone. She will still be waiting at 9p.m. or later if he hasn't called yet, not engaging with other friends or family members in fear of missing his call. If this happens once, there may be a reasonable explanation. But when this becomes a pattern of behavior, it has evolved into a situation of power and control; much more than an innocent missed phone call.

(2) Isolation

Similar to adult relationships, teen boyfriends want their girlfriends to be isolated from others so they are more dependant on them. For the girlfriend, the embarrassment of the situation and her belief that nobody would understand it cause her to become even more isolated. He may make her feel guilty for being with friends and even family. Many times, teens in this situation will lose interest in other activities and stop spending time with their friends altogether. They find that upsetting their boyfriend just isn't worth it.

(3) Jealousy Issues

Teens are typically insecure and uncertain about peer-to-peer relationships, not to mention dating relationships. Add abuse into the equation and you have a recipe for disaster. Oftentimes, teen boyfriends are extremely jealous of their girlfriends and possessive of their time and attention. They don't want her talking to or spending time with other people, especially other boys.

(4) Name Calling and Criticism

This can be the most destructive type of abuse in teen relationships. The boyfriend will put his girlfriend down, especially in front of others, call her names, tell her she is fat, be critical of decisions she makes, tell her she is crazy, criticize her clothes, hair and looks. He may say things like, "You're so lucky to have me as your boyfriend because nobody else would want you." Or "I'm the best you're going to get." It's degrading and demeaning, but exactly what he is trying to accomplish – ripping apart her self-esteem so she will not leave.

(5) Violent Behavior

As we see in adult abusers, teen abusers have quick and short tempers. They are easily angered and situations escalate quickly. She may not know what set him off, but that hardly matters. He is still upset and she is going to nurture and try to pacify him. Girls who grew up in abusive homes are extremely proficient in reading facial expressions of their loved ones. It is part of the survival skills she developed so she could assess the situation between her mother and father and determine how to respond. Because of this, all it takes from a boyfriend is "the look" which communicates volumes without him ever lifting a hand. It is also very possible that she has witnessed him being violent with other people or animals. (Violence with animals often progresses to violence with humans as it desensitizes the abuser.)

(6) Emotional Changes

Has the girl in a new relationship suddenly changed? Was she previously a fun-loving, outgoing person who is now quiet and withdrawn? Does she seem secretive? Does she still hang out with her friends? Or is it all about the boyfriend? Any of these changes could be indicators of an unhealthy dating relationship. As tempting as it is for teens in a new relationship to spend all of their time with their new boyfriend or girlfriend, it is completely unhealthy. Seeing how they interact with each other in group settings can be very telling. How do they treat each other? Are they jealous if one person talks to someone else?

(7) Making Excuses

It is very common for girls to defend their abusive boyfriends. Even though they are being victimized, they feel the need to protect them. The girls make excuses for their boyfriends' behavior to their family and friends, saying things like "You don't know how hard of a life he's had" or "It's not as bad as it seems, you're just blowing it out of proportion."

(8) Physical Signs

As with adult abusive relationships, teen abusive relationships have a progression of violence. They start out full of emotional and verbal abuse, but without intervention they will lead to physical violence. You may see scratches, bruises or other injuries that don't have a reasonable explanation. Physical abuse could involve hitting, beating, shoving, pushing, forcefully restraining her, or even roughhousing or play wrestling that is just a little too physical.

Teen dating violence is increasing in frequency. It is something to be taken seriously and although it has many similarities to adult abuse, there are differences as well. It is likely that girls will need help in developing an exit strategy for getting out of the relationship as well as a safety plan to keep her safe from her abuser. It's possible that she will need medical, legal and psychological assistance and also help getting it. Putting an end to teen dating violence is an important step in fighting family violence. Children are learning abuse in their homes and taking it with them into their relationships as they grow into adulthood. The perpetuating cycle doesn't have to repeat if some are willing to get help and others are willing to intervene.

Chapter Summary

- One in five teens that have been in a serious dating relationship have been hit, slapped or pushed by their partner.

- Power and control in teen relationships is very similar to that in adult relationships.

- The Teen Power and Control Wheel and the Teen Relationship Equality Wheel can be used side-by-side as a tool with teens in an abusive relationship to highlight problem areas.

- There are several warning signs to help identify an abusive teen relationship:
    - Constant communication
    - Isolation
    - Jealousy issues
    - Name calling and criticism
    - Violent behavior
    - Emotional changes
    - Making excuses
    - Physical Signs

http://www.youtube.com/watch?v=kxoDEns7wlg

Chapter Questions

(1) What is teen dating violence? How is it different from adult abusive relationships?

(2) List 3 differences between the teen power and control wheel and the adult version.

(3) List 3 similarities between the teen power and control wheel and the adult wheel.

(4) What is the teen equality wheel?

(5) List and describe the eight signs of teen dating violence.

Chapter 4: Family Violence Laws

History of Family Violence Laws

The first documented U.S. court case regarding child abuse was recorded in 1874. Although no child abuse laws existed at the time, there were laws concerning cruelty to animals. It was under these laws that the case was brought before the court. The American Society for the Prevention of Cruelty to Animals successfully argued that the child in this case was protected under the laws that prevented the mistreatment of animals.

Shortly after the success of this case, over 200 Societies for the Prevention of Cruelty to Children opened around the country and states began passing laws against child abuse. Unfortunately, child abuse didn't become a major concern in society for another 80+ years. Child abuse, much like family violence, was considered to be a private matter that was best handled behind closed doors. It was rare for anyone to intercede on behalf of the victim; and if someone did, it was usually a family member or the local pastor. The issue was reported to authorities infrequently and even more uncommon was it for a child to be removed from the home.

It wasn't until the 1960s when the first mandatory child abuse reporting laws began to change things. Instead of a taboo family secret, child abuse was suddenly something that demanded the public's attention as reports from doctors and school officials brought the issue to the limelight. In 1974, Congress passed the Child Abuse Prevention and Treatment Act (CAPTA). CAPTA allowed for federal funds to be given to states that passed mandatory reporting laws. Today all 50 states have such laws.

As the awareness of and willingness to address child abuse grew, the spotlight soon shifted to include victims of partner abuse as well. The feminist movement of the 1960s also helped open the door for this issue to be addressed. However, it wasn't without much societal consternation. Remember, for hundreds of years, family violence was a private matter. So when shelters started opening and people started speaking out against family violence, they were met with some resistance. Many people still believed that women were unintentionally provoking the abuse or in some way contributing to it.

As some of the ground-breaking researchers who had previously tackled the child abuse issue got involved, they started to help shift public opinion on the issue. They approached the issue from a scientific and sociological perspective rather than a personal and emotional one. Research was done on the issue and public awareness grew until the passage of the Violence Against Women Act (VAWA) in 1994. The high profile murder of Nicole Brown Simpson, former wife of NFL star O.J. Simpson, assisted in bringing awareness to the issue. Family violence was suddenly in the forefront of the media as people realized that if violence could happen to celebrities, it could happen to anyone. It also brought to light that family violence included elder abuse, same-sex partner abuse and dating violence.

 http://www.youtube.com/watch?v=MlzlvyCQpwE

Violence Against Women Act (VAWA)

 http://www.youtube.com/watch?v=baDAJdC-r9I

VAWA was the first comprehensive federal legislation to address violence against women in the United States. It was first passed in 1994 with improvements and revisions made in 2000 and again in 2005. The goal of VAWA is geared toward improving our country's response to domestic violence, sexual assault, stalking and teen dating violence. It provides funding to help children exposed to violence, transitional housing for women escaping abusive homes, training for health care providers to support victims, provide crisis intervention services for victims as well as training for law enforcement officials and judges.

Crime Codes

While most laws related to family violence are state laws, there are also some laws at the national level. At the state level, the laws include specifics about threats, stalking, restraining orders, assault, endangerment, kidnapping, harassment, unlawful imprisonment, and sexual offenses. At the federal level, there are laws regarding immigration, family violence on military bases, and guns.

It is important to be familiar with the laws in the state where you reside. Specific areas to research include domestic violence, restraining orders, criminal threats, harassment, kidnapping, elder abuse, sexual assault and child abuse.

Departmental Policies

Many police departments have implemented departmental policies which are the agency's specific protocol for handling various situations. These policies include protocols for handling family violence cases. They might include the necessity of interviewing children or require that officers obtain an Emergency Protective Order on every family violence arrest. Some agencies even require that some type of report (even if it is only an information report) is taken on every call for service for family violence. Also included in these policies are arrest protocols and guidelines for confiscating weapons for safekeeping. The important thing is that officers are aware of their department's specific protocols and requirements.

http://www.youtube.com/watch?v=3s2hu9Zon4s

Chapter Summary

- The first documented U.S. court case regarding child abuse was recorded in 1874. Because no laws against child abuse existed, the case was prosecuted under animal cruelty laws.

- In 1994, the Violence Against Women Act was passed making it the first comprehensive federal legislation to address violence against women in the United States.

- Laws against family violence exist at both the national level and the state level.

- Many police departments have implemented departmental policies which are the agency's specific protocol for handing various situations.

Chapter Questions

(1) What is CAPTA?

(2) What high profile case led to the passage of VAWA?

(3) What is VAWA? And what is its purpose?

(4) Look up and list the sections of the penal codes of your state that correspond with the following crimes:

- Spousal abuse

- Child abuse

- Violation of restraining order

- Stalking

- Criminal threats

- Spousal rape

Chapter 5: Injuries

Common Injuries

Since family violence is such a volatile situation, varying injuries can occur by anyone involved. Injuries can range from something minor such as a scratch to something very serious like a gunshot wound. Not all injuries are physical in appearance and internal injuries are often overlooked. It's important to document any injury and officers should even go as far as listing any pain an individual is feeling. Using the proper terminology to describe an injury is crucial. Calling a laceration a scratch could have an adverse effect on the outcome of a case. Listed below are definitions of visible and non-visible injuries that are commonly sustained and encountered.

- **Visible Injuries:**
    - *Welts* - a raised ridge or lump on skin caused by a blow and/or trauma
    - *Bruises* - a pool of blood under the skin caused by blood leaking from damaged capillaries usually from some type of blunt trauma
    - *Scratches* - a slight wound or very shallow cut in the top layer of skin

- *Bite marks* - an impression caused by teeth whether or not the skin is punctured
- *Lacerations* - a deep rip, cut or tear into the many layers of skin
- *Abrasions* - a scraped area on skin
- *Stab wounds* - a puncture or punctures caused by a sharp object
- *Gunshot wounds* - a puncture in the skin caused by a projectile from a gun
- *Swelling* - an enlarged area of the body caused by some sort of trauma
- *Redness* - (inflammation) a response from the body tissues as a result of injury or irritation characterized by pain, swelling, and/or heat
- *Bumps* - (bulge) a raised rounded spot or lump

The following clip features a child abuse crime scene investigation that contains some of the above injuries and shows how they are dealt with in the field.

http://www.youtube.com/watch?v=BbkVdpwW2jM

Examples of Visible Injuries

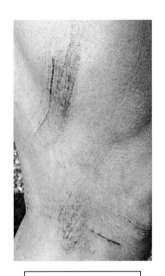

Abrasion

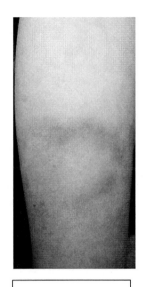

Bite mark

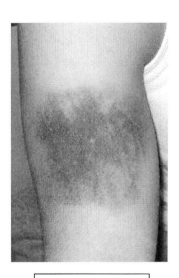

Bruise

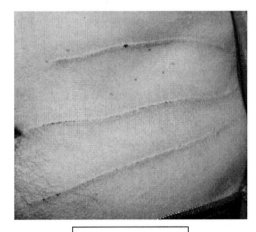

Scratches

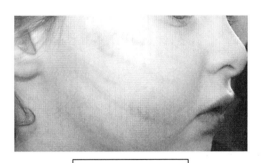

Welts

- **Non-visible Injuries:**
  - *Broken bones* - a break, rupture, or crack in bone or cartilage
  - *Soft tissue injuries* - pain, inflammation, and/or strain of the various tissues in the body
  - *Internal injuries* - damage to internal organs of the body
  - *Hemorrhaging* - an excessive discharge of blood from the blood vessels; profuse bleeding

Julie was an outgoing, popular woman with a jealous and controlling boyfriend named Israel. In fact, two weeks ago Julie ended their nine month relationship because of his overbearing and jealous behaviors. Israel called Julie several times trying to reconcile, but Julie was done giving him "chances" and was ready to move on with her life. Israel heard from mutual friends that Julie had moved on and was interested in dating, but he wasn't convinced that she was over him. He kept calling her, begging her to give him another chance.

One night, while Julie was at home watching TV, Israel started pounding on her door demanding her to open it so they could talk. Julie refused to open it and told him through the door to go away and leave her alone because their relationship was over. Israel kicked in the door, causing the door jamb to break, and grabbed Julie by the hair. Julie began screaming as Israel dragged her out of the house towards his car. When Israel opened the car door and tried to force her into the car, Julie fought back, kicking and hitting Israel. Israel told Julie that if she didn't get into the car, he was going to kill her, but Julie continued to struggle until she broke free from his grasp. She ran down the street screaming for help when Israel jumped into the driver's seat of his car to chase her down. Julie was running towards her parents' house who lived two blocks over when she crossed the street, and Israel accelerated his vehicle, veering towards Stacy, running her over. He left significant tire impressions across her torso and, without stopping, drove away. Israel was found and taken into custody several hours later.

Primary Aggressor

The primary aggressor is the person determined to be the *most significant* aggressor, not necessarily the *first* aggressor. This is an important distinction to make as many times an abuser may claim that the victim "started it". However, if one party slaps the other, and a punch to the face is given in return, it is likely to conclude that the second party will be assessed as the primary aggressor rather than the person who "started it" with a slap.

In determining the primary aggressor, the responding officer should consider all factors. A comprehensive, but non-conclusive list follows:

- The intent of the law to protect victims from continuing abuse
- Presence of fear (and who is fearful of whom)
- History of violence between the parties involved
- Whether either person involved acted in self-defense
- Current or previous orders of protection filed against either party
- Height and weight of the parties involved (including strength and skill)
- 911 reporting party
- Use of alcohol or drugs
- Motivation of one party to lie or retaliate
- The corroboration of injuries, evidence and statements of both parties

Again, this list is not intended to be all-inclusive, but rather a tool for jumpstarting an investigation.

Defensive Injuries

Defensive injuries are found when a victim tries to fight off her attacker and the injuries she causes are considered to be made in self-defense.

When both parties have injuries, it may be challenging for a first responder to accurately determine the primary aggressor. It is important to understand, defensive injuries are different types of injuries and care should be taken to assess what type of injuries each person possesses.

Wounds on the victim's palms and hands are found when she is fighting off her attacker and puts her hands up in front of her face in defense of an oncoming blow. Wounds on the inside and outside of a victim's arms could be the result of the abuser grabbing her forcefully. Bumps on a victim's head, especially the back of the head, can be a result of being thrown up against a wall, or pinned down on the ground. Bite marks on the perpetrator's chest, biceps and forearms can be the result of a victim fighting back, being held against her will or even rape. Scratches on the perpetrator's face, chest and neck are also considered defensive injuries.

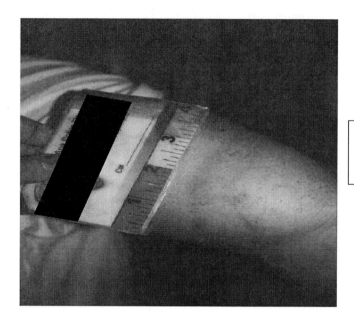

A Victim's injury the day of the incident – her Boyfriend grabbed her by the arm

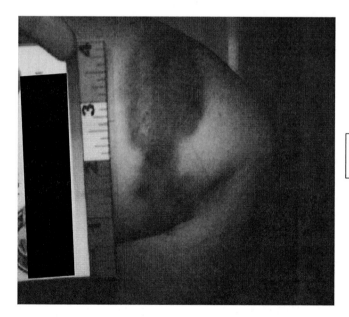

The same victim's injury 2 days after the incident

GROUP ACTIVITY

Break into small groups of 3-4 people. Read the following scenario and respond as if you were a police officer.

You receive a call to respond to a domestic violence incident at the hospital. Melissa, a 20 year old female, states that she and Alex, her 22 year old boyfriend of six years and the father of her 3 children, just had a physical altercation. Melissa says Alex asked her for a ride to pick up his car, which he had left at a friend's house. Their 3 children rode with them from their house in National City to the friend's house in Lexington. During their drive, Alex and Melissa began to argue about Alex's drug use. As they arrived at the friend's house, the verbal argument grew into a physical altercation. Melissa says she became irate and slapped Alex in the arm as he was driving. She says she hit him with minimal force and it was only to attract his attention. Alex responded by punching her in the face with his right fist. Melissa immediately began to bleed. Melissa then told Alex she wanted to go home. Once at home, they dropped off their children and Alex then drove Melissa to the hospital. Alex says he and Melissa got into an argument about his drug use. He admits to being addicted to methamphetamines since the age of 15. He says that their argument became physical today because she slapped him on the face. He admits to striking her in the mouth. He also says he felt sorry after they dropped their kids off and that is why he brought her to the hospital. Melissa has visible injuries: a lacerated and bloodied lip and a chipped front tooth.

Questions:
    (1) Identify victim(s) and suspect.
    (2) Identify potential injuries.
    (3) Identify and list crime violations.
    (4) Outline your course of action.

Strangulation

Most people don't understand that there is a significant difference between strangulation and choking. Although the words are often used interchangeably, they should not be because they are not the same thing. Strangling is the compression of the neck by an outside force; choking is an internal obstruction of the flow of air from the environment.

Strangulation can be difficult to detect as there are frequently little or no *immediate* signs of injury. However, minor injuries may be present. They could include red marks, scratches and/or bruising on the neck. Victims will also sometimes complain of throat pain, hoarseness, difficulty swallowing, voice changes, persistent pain, and difficulty breathing. Another sign of strangulation is petechiae hemorrhaging. These are small red or purple dots caused by a minor hemorrhage (broken capillary blood vessels). They can be found in or around the eyes. In severe cases, it is possible to view significant blood in the whites of the eyes of strangulation victims.

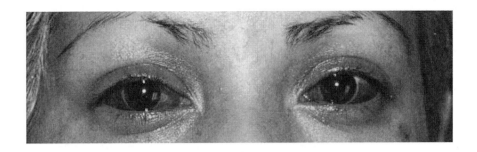

> The whites of this victim's eyes are filled with blood indicating a prolonged and very serious incident.

The challenge with strangulation cases is that while there may be minimal visible injuries immediately after the incident, it is likely that visible injuries will appear after a few hours, days and even weeks. There are documented cases of strangulation victims dying up to several weeks later due to brain damage caused by a lack of oxygen, compression of the carotid artery, trachea or larynx, internal bleeding, or a fractured or broken hyoid bone.

In strangulation cases, it is especially important to not only take photographs at the time of the incident, but also to schedule follow-up photos for 2-3 days later. Victims are also strongly encouraged to seek medical attention to rule out the possibility of delayed reaction to the strangulation.

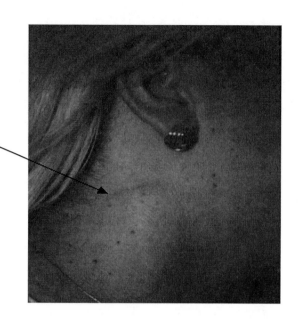

Examples of minor strangulation injury

Chapter Summary

- Varying Injuries occur and can range from a scratch to a gunshot wound.
- Not all injuries are physical in appearance and internal injuries are often overlooked.
- The primary aggressor is the person determined to be the *most significant* aggressor, not necessarily the *first* aggressor.
- Defensive injuries are found when a victim tries to fight off her attacker and the injuries she causes are considered to be made in self-defense.
- There is a significant difference between strangulation and choking: the former is an external force and the latter is an internal obstruction.
- Strangulation can be difficult to detect as there are frequently little or no *immediate* signs of injury.

Chapter Questions

(1) How is the primary aggressor determined?

(2) What are defensive injuries? List three examples.

(3) What is the difference between strangulation and choking?

(4) What are three signs that strangulation occurred?

(5) What are petechiae hemorrhaging?

Chapter 6: Stalking

Stacey was a beautiful 28 year-old woman who had been dating John for close to two years. When Stacey realized that she didn't really want to marry John, she decided that it would be best to break up with him. John was really upset and begged her not to break up with him. She felt like it was the right thing to do, so she stayed strong in her decision. A few days later, John started "showing up" everywhere Stacey was – the grocery store, the bank, at the restaurant where she was eating with her friends, the post office, etc. At first it seemed like coincidences. After all, they had been together for a couple of years and developed similar habits and favorite places to go. But after awhile, Stacey realized it couldn't just be coincidence. John also started leaving notes on her car telling her how much he loved her, begging her to take him back, and telling her how he "just couldn't live without her".

Stacey was concerned about her safety and because of his notes and his threats, she filed a restraining order against him. When I met Stacey, it had been 2 months since she had the restraining order in place. She had called the police over a dozen times to report restraining order violations. She had a large Ziploc bag full of notes and letters from John. The notes were from the past week alone! By now, they had not seen each other for several months and Stacey had started dating someone new. John seemed to be particularly upset by this and Stacey had seen an escalation in his behavior since the new boyfriend came on the scene. The new boyfriend was starting to get annoyed with the old boyfriend and the "hassle" of always calling the police, delivering evidence to the District Attorney's office, etc. He was beginning to wonder if the relationship with Stacey was worth all the extra work and "baggage" that came with it.

The District Attorney prosecuted John for the restraining order violations and was successful in her case. John was sent to jail for several months. Stacey took the time while he was incarcerated to move out of her apartment and reestablish herself in a new area that would be unfamiliar to John. She wanted more distance from John than the restraining order provided (since John wouldn't abide by it) and she wanted a chance at the relationship with her new boyfriend. Although she was frustrated that she was the one who had to move to a different city and change everything about her daily life, she knew it was the only way to be free of John.

Unfortunately, Stacey's story is a familiar one. While we most often hear about celebrities who are being stalked by crazy fans, these types of cases only account for 15% of all reported stalking cases. "Celebrity stalkers" are also a different type of stalker. They are fixated on their subject, but they don't often become physically violent. Family violence stalkers on the other hand, are certainly the most dangerous and lethal type of stalker.

Surprisingly, stalking is a fairly "new" crime. After a series of high profile cases, California became the first state in the United States to criminalize stalking in 1990. Within three years, every state had done the same to create laws against stalking. While all states recognize stalking as a crime, the definition of stalking varies across jurisdiction and some states lack proper penalties for violating this law. In addition, many law enforcement personnel do not understand their state's anti-stalking laws nor does much of the public understand that stalking is a crime. In spite of the misperceptions and differences in definitions, the U.S. Department of Justice estimates there are more than 2 million felony and 4 million misdemeanor stalking cases each year.

The Department of Justice defines stalking "as a course of conduct directed at a specific person that would cause a reasonable person to feel fear". The decisions police officers make at the scene, the information they document, and their description of the victim's demeanor significantly impact what charges a prosecutor is able to file against the offending party. Understanding the dynamics at play between the stalker and his victim are crucial to the victim's safety and an effective prosecution of the case.

The Impact of Stalking on its Victims

Stalking victims live in constant fear. Stalkers are incredibly unpredictable and that is how they wield control over their victims without being in their lives on a daily basis. Their victims are left feeling helpless, angry, and fearful and suffer in a variety of ways. It is common for victims to experience weight loss, sleep disturbances, nightmares, anxiety attacks, depression, memory loss, and a myriad of other physical and emotional symptoms.

- Fear of: what the stalker will do next, who is at the door, leaving the house, the delivery man, being home alone
- Anxiety about: the safety of family members and pets, whether or not the stalking will end, how other people will respond to the situation if they know what is happening
- Vulnerability: feeling completely exposed, never feeling safe, not knowing who to trust or where to turn for help
- Nervousness: jumpy, irritable, impatient, on edge, being startled by small things

- Depression: feeling despair, hopelessness, tearful, angry
- Hyper-vigilance: being continually alert to known and unknown dangers, taking elaborate safety measures against the stalker *and* any suspicious people, repeatedly checking door / window locks
- Physical ailments: stomach aches, nausea, headaches, eating problems
- Flashbacks: reliving frightening incidents
- Sleeping problems: nightmares, interrupted sleep patterns, insomnia, sleeping all the time
- Isolation: disconnecting from family or friends
- Abusing drugs and/or alcohol: to numb fear and anxiety or to induce calm or sleep

Many stalking victims do not seek help. They are afraid of how the stalker will respond once law enforcement intervenes and quite honestly, victims think they know the stalker well enough to be able to predict his behavior. Because a relationship between the two did exist, the victim knows what her abuser is capable of doing to her.

http://www.youtube.com/watch?v=P8Pc6GEUfZ0&list=PL602B5AC106B3C11B&feature=plpp

Assistance for Stalking Victims

 http://www.youtube.com/watch?v=Deq-EwLGVpk

Victims of domestic violence related stalking cases are unique. They have limited resources available to them and they are slow in seeking help. However, the best place for victims to look is the National Center for Victims of Crime. They provide comprehensive resources for victims of many different crimes, including stalking. Victims may also seek advice from a professional victim advocate. They are trained to assist crime victims with staying safe, writing a personalized safety plan, referrals to emergency shelters and/or counselors, applying for restraining orders, moving, filing a police report and more.

Stalking victims are strongly encouraged to take simple safety precautions:

- Vary daily routine
- Change travel routes (e.g. don't travel the same way and/or from work)
- Ride with friends to and from work
- Go with other parents to pick-up and drop-off children

- Leave home and work at a different time each day

- Shop and run errands with someone else

- Spend free time outside of the home with other people

- Protect personal information (e.g. shred mail before discarding, be wary of unsolicited inquiries, search for yourself on the internet to see how much information is available)

Writing and following a safety plan can increase a stalking victim's safety. It is important for victims to think through both short- and long-term options well in advance such as knowing how to get help in an emergency. A safety plan should also include a place for emergency shelter in case the victim has to leave home without warning. A thorough plan would involve temporary and permanent options. A critical aspect of safety planning is minimizing contact with the stalker. The victim should never initiate contact with the stalker (unless it is to notify him of a petition for restraining order).

Victims can also play a role in collecting evidence against their stalker. The easiest way to do this is to keep a written log of all stalking-related incidents including the date, time and place the incident occurred. It is also helpful to record thoughts and feelings at the time of the incident. Victims should also keep any letters, packages, photos, videos or voicemail messages to submit to the police. Because many commercial properties, such as gas stations and malls, have a surveillance system, victims can request copies of the tapes which may contain evidence of stalking. Anything the victim documents and/or collects can support the accusation of harassment and stalking.

It can be easy for a victim to think that she has to handle all of this on her own. She may also feel a sense of responsibility to protect the people around her from also becoming victims. However, the sooner the crime is reported to the police the better it is. *All* incidents, however big or small, should be reported to the police. I've had victims tell me they only reported the "big" incidents or the really "scary" ones. But every small incident that is documented helps paint a bigger picture of what is actually happening to the victim. If a victim has been intimidated or doesn't think law enforcement can help, talking with a victim advocate might be a good place to start.

Finally, it is critical that stalking victims consider getting a restraining order against their stalker. Any physical or sexual assault, damage to property, or threats may be grounds for gaining a retraining order. While orders of protection are not guarantees of safety, they can be a deterrent to the stalker who fears the possible consequences of a violation. Restraining orders also help law enforcement because the stalker can be arrested for violating the order before a more serious altercation occurs.

Whatever course of action the victim chooses to take is just that...her choice. While law enforcement officials and victim advocates are available to help her, it is ultimately the victim who has to deal with any consequences that may occur as a result of calling the police, filing a restraining order or going into an emergency shelter. As stated earlier, family violence stalkers are the most violent and dangerous offenders. Victims do know their abusers better than anyone and usually have an idea of which course of action will be helpful and which one will not.

In one recent case, Bill left his wife, Meredith, for his mistress and filed for a divorce. While she was at first shocked and devastated, Meredith eventually snapped out of her depression and began living again. She realized that she hadn't really been happy with Bill and this was her chance to live her life the way she wanted to. She even started dating again and was seeing a wonderful man.

When things didn't work out with his mistress, Bill wanted Meredith back. She of course said "no." Bill became relentless in his pursuit of her, showing up at her work, sending her letters, leaving notes and flowers on her car, etc. When the tone of the notes became more frightening, Meredith filed for and obtained a restraining order against Bill. Unfortunately, he constantly violated the restraining order and was arrested several times. At one point, Bill told their older children that

Meredith would not see December. On November 30th, in a crowded shopping mall parking lot, Bill killed Meredith and her boyfriend. After wounding them, Bill stood over each of them, reloaded his weapon and shot them both in the head several times.

This is a particularly sad story as Meredith did everything she could have done to protect herself from Bill. She changed daily routines, worked with a victim advocate, reported all incidents to police and filed for a restraining order. It is hard to know what will cause one person to go as far as murder while another can be stopped with a restraining order. The most important thing you can do to help a victim is to encourage her to follow all necessary steps for her to be a safe as possible.

Carol Cromer shares her story of survivorship after stalking and attacks.

   http://www.youtube.com/watch?v=r1Cge6wHBOg

Chapter Summary

- California became the first state to criminalize stalking in 1990 after a serious of high profile stalking cases.

- The U.S. Department of Justice estimates there are more than 6 million stalking cases each year.

- Stalking has a significant impact on its victims and most victims do not seek help.

- Stalking victims are strongly encouraged to take simple safety precautions.

- Restraining orders are an important tool for stalking victims to utilize against their stalker.

Chapter Questions

(1) Stalking was criminalized in 1990 due to several high profile cases that occurred in California. Research the high profile cases that led to this and describe one of them including the case name, a summary of the case, and the outcome.

(2) Describe three unique ways stalking victims are impacted by their stalkers.

(3) Describe four simple safety precautions a victim can take.

(4) What are five resources available for stalking victims?

Chapter 7: Family Violence Investigations

Misdemeanor Cases and Why They are Important

In the past, police officers were hesitant to respond to calls for service that involved incidents of family violence. Since it was a "private" matter, officers were instructed to make sure the situation was deescalated and then leave. Today things are much different and most state laws mandate officers not only respond, but document the incident.

There are two types of crimes: misdemeanors and felonies. Misdemeanors are considered "lesser" crimes and the punishment is less severe. Felonies are considered to be more serious in nature and can be violent or non-violent, but carry a much stricter punishment than misdemeanors. Oftentimes, a pattern of misdemeanors can be a precursor for felonious behavior and this is also the case with incidents of family violence. Statistically, abuse worsens over time if the couple stays together. Prosecutors will use prior misdemeanor cases to help prove a current case.

Misdemeanors are less obviously serious crimes and there are frequently no prior reported incidents of abuse. Sadly, it is common for victims to recant their stories after the incident. Recanting victims do not make prosecution impossible, but it definitely makes it difficult. Victims recant for many reasons some of which include:

- feeling responsible for what happened

- being afraid of retaliation

- feeling afraid of the consequences of prosecution

 http://www.youtube.com/watch?v=C5nXA1L-yNM

How Investigation Helps at Trial

How the first responder handles the scene of a misdemeanor will make or break the case. In all cases, but particularly with misdemeanors, photos can lead to the case being filed with the district attorney or dismissed altogether. Because victims usually recant almost immediately after reporting the incident, the sooner the injuries are photographed, the better. Many times the officer may ask the victim to come to the station a few days later for follow-up photos, and while she may agree at the scene with the best of intentions, she will seldom follow through.

Diane and her boyfriend Tom had lived together for several years. They had what they both described as a volatile relationship with frequent heated arguments. On this particular day, Diane's neighbors called the police to report the fight. Diane and Tom had been arguing when Tom grabbed her by the shoulders and head-butted Diane. She got scared and ran out the back door of the house, jumping over backyard fences until she was far enough away that Tom couldn't catch her. When the neighbors saw her running through the yards, they called the police. By the time the officers arrived at the house, Diane was back home where she and Tom were making up from their fight.

Tom told the officers it was a simple disagreement and they were working things out. Officers observed a large egg-shaped bruise on Diane's forehead. In addition, they noticed that her clothes were torn in various places. When pressed, Diane told the officers what happened and that her clothes were ripped while she was jumping over the fences. She also stated that she had various bruises on her arms and legs, both from Tom and from the fences. In addition, she said that both she and Tom had been drinking which had probably escalated the argument.

Officers arrested Tom for domestic violence and called a crime scene investigator to document the injuries and damage to the house. They also encouraged Diane to call the detectives who would be assigned to her case in 2-3 days so they could take follow-up photographs of her injuries. I met Diane when she came in for the follow-up photos. Even though she had come in for the photos, she also wanted to talk to the detectives about dropping the case against her boyfriend. She explained to me that she was drunk during the argument and when she was running away from Tom, she ran into a wall which caused the "goose egg" on her forehead.

After going around and around about what actually happened, including a demonstration to Diane to show her that it was virtually impossible to get a goose egg on her forehead from running into a wall unless she had been running sideways, Diane finally relented and said she just wanted Tom to get out of jail and come back home. She felt guilty because she had been drinking and thought she had instigated the argument. She felt like she deserved the abuse because she wouldn't listen to him and drank too much. I tried to explain to her that regardless of what she did wrong, she still didn't deserve to be hit. It was difficult, and virtually impossible, convincing a woman who had grown up in an abusive home and had spent several years with an abusive boyfriend that abuse isn't a part of every relationship. In the end all I could do was support her by appearing in court with her, encourage her to get counseling (both for the physical abuse and the alcohol abuse) and give her resources to help both her and Tom have a healthier relationship. The decision of what to do with all the information was completely hers.

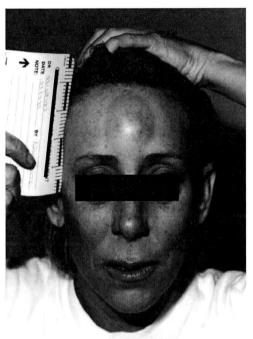

Diane's injury the day of the incident – notice the large egg shaped bump and bruise in the center of her forehead. The bruise was a pale shade of purple and green.

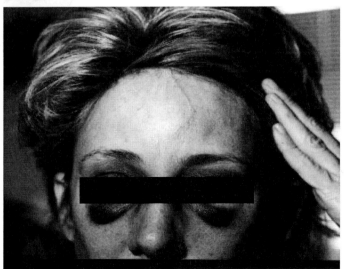

Diane's injury 3 days later. The injury to her forehead drained into her eyes, bruising around her eyes and pooling below her eyes in a shade of dark purple.

Any time that a crime scene investigator can be called, the better it is for the case. They are able to document the scene in a way that the officers and other first responders (such as a victim advocate) will not be able to do. Photographs of any other evidence (such as broken dishes, overturned furniture, etc.) is extremely helpful to corroborate the stories of the victim and the suspect, either proving or disproving what was said. Whenever possible, it is helpful to collect any physical evidence such as phones ripped out of the wall, broken items, and torn clothing. And if something can't be collected, such as a punched wall, take a picture. After all, we all know that a picture is worth a thousand words!

911 tapes are also very helpful at trial because they can corroborate the version of events the victim (or the suspect) told the reporting officer. They will also show that the victim was under the stress of the event and therefore telling the truth at the time the incident was reported. Finally, they will show the jury (if a jury trial takes place) and the court the seriousness of the crime that was committed. Oftentimes it is the children who call the police and it is a very powerful account of what was actually happening in the house which is difficult for the suspect to refute.

Report Writing

While it is important for the first responder to properly handle the call for service, it is equally as important for him or her to write a thorough report capturing as much information as possible. Because victims often recant, the report becomes central to the case. In fact, in many states, there is an evidence code section that allows the officer to testify to a victim's out of court statements in which the victim or witness is still under the stress of an event. What does this mean specifically? If a victim is crying, upset, angry, or otherwise demonstrably emotionally affected by the event, the officer can testify as to what she said to him or her. This is extremely important because victims are usually uncooperative by the time of the trial and this may be the only way to prove a case.

Victim and suspect information should always be completed fully. This includes names, dates of birth, identification numbers, employer information, related address or phone numbers, etc. If a victim says she is going to a friend or relative's home, document the address and phone number of where she is going.

The physical descriptions of both parties involved should also be documented. Especially if the victim is in hiding or uncooperative by the time the case is in court, as it is helpful to know the size differential between the two parties. For example, if the victim is a 100 lb. 5'4" female and the defendant is a 195 lb. 6'2" male OR conversely, if the victim is a small male and the defendant is a large female, it could make a difference in the case's viability in court.

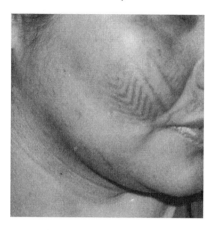

Shoeprint
on a
victim's cheek

Documentation of injuries is critical. All injuries should be photographed and documented as to color, size and location. All injuries include those to the victim and to the suspect and should include a narrative detailing how the injuries were received. Matching visible injuries with evidence at the scene will also assist in prosecution. For example, find the shoe that made the print on the victim's cheek below and book it into evidence. (Further specifics of injury documentation will be discussed in more detail in Chapter 8.)

On the following pages is an example of a specialized domestic violence report form:

DOMESTIC VIOLENCE REPORT

LOCATION OF INCIDENT			TIME OCCURRED	TIME REPORTED

CODES: V- Victim S- Suspect (primary aggressor) P - Involved Party Only

CODE	#	NAME	LAST, FIRST, MIDDLE	DOB	SEX	RACE	CDL OR ID CARD NUMBER
		HOME ADDRSS INCLUDE ZIP CODE		PHONE NUMBER	HEIGHT	WEIGHT	HAIR	EYES

CODE	#	NAME	LAST, FIRST, MIDDLE	DOB	SEX	RACE	CDL OR ID CARD NUMBER
		HOME ADDRSS INCLUDE ZIP CODE		PHONE NUMBER	HEIGHT	WEIGHT	HAIR	EYES

RELATIONSHIP OF INVOLVED PARTIES
(Mark all that apply)

☐ Married
☐ Divorced
☐ Cohabitants
☐ Former Co-Habitants
☐ Dating
☐ Formerly Dating

☐ Same Sex
☐ Emancipated Minor
☐ Engaged
☐ Child from Relationship
   # of children: ____

Duration of Relationship: Years ____ Months ____

EXISTING RESTRAINING ORDERS

Issued? ☐ YES ☐ NO
Issuing Court: _____
Order/Docket # _____

On file? ☐ YES ☐ NO
PD Case # _____
Agency: _____

☐ Current
☐ Expired
☐ Emergency
☐ Temporary
☐ Permanent
☐ Other: ____

CONDITION OF VICTIM

☐ Angry
☐ Apologetic
☐ Crying
☐ Fearful
☐ Hysterical
☐ Calm
☐ Pregnant
☐ Irrational
☐ Nervous
☐ Threatening
☐ Complaint of Pain

☐ Bruise
☐ Abrasion/Scratches
☐ Minor Cut
☐ Laceration
☐ Fracture
☐ Concussion
☐ Drinking/Drugs
☐ Strangulation
☐ Other/ Explain: ____

CONDITION OF SUSPECT

☐ Angry
☐ Apologetic
☐ Crying
☐ Fearful
☐ Hysterical
☐ Calm
☐ Pregnant
☐ Irrational
☐ Nervous
☐ Threatening
☐ Complaint of Pain

☐ Bruise
☐ Abrasion/Scratches
☐ Minor Cut
☐ Laceration
☐ Fracture
☐ Concussion
☐ Drinking/Drugs
☐ Strangulation
☐ Other/ Explain: ____

MEDICAL TREATMENT (VICTIM)

☐ None
☐ First Aid
☐ Paramedics

☐ Hospital
☐ Will see own Doctor
☐ Refused Medical Aid

Medic Name/ID:

Medic Name/ID:

Hospital:

Attending Physician:

MEDICAL TREATMENT (SUSPECT)

☐ None
☐ First Aid
☐ Paramedics

☐ Hospital
☐ Will see own Doctor
☐ Refused Medical Aid

Medic Name/ID:

Medic Name/ID:

Hospital:

Attending Physician:

REPORTING OFFICER	ID#	DATE	TIME	DISTRICT	WATCH

HISTORY

Prior History of Domestic Violence? ☐ YES ☐ NO
Prior History of Violence Documented? ☐ YES ☐ NO
Number of Prior Incidents: _____
Investigating Agency: _____
Case # (s) _____

WITNESSES

Witnesses present during DV? ☐ YES ☐ NO
Statements taken? ☐ YES ☐ NO
Children present during DV? ☐ YES ☐ NO
Name(s) and Age(s) of Children:

WEAPONS INVOLVED (check all that apply)

☐ Open Hand   ☐ Shoes/Boots
☐ Closed Fist   ☐ Other
☐ Firearm   List: _____
  Type:
☐ Knife   _____
  Type: _____

Weapon seized? ☐ YES ☐ NO   · Evidence? ☐ YES ☐ NO
72 hour hold? ☐ YES ☐ NO   OK to release? ☐ YES ☐ NO

Party # _____ prohibited from   YES ☐ NO ☐
owning per PC 12021?   CII #:

WITNESSES/CONTACTS
(In criminal cases, you must list name and address of victim's nearest relative)

CODE	#	NAME	LAST, FIRST, MIDDLE	DOB	CDL OR ID CARD NUMBER		
			HOME ADDRSS INCLUDE ZIP CODE		PHONE NUMBER	SEX	RACE
CODE	#	NAME	LAST, FIRST, MIDDLE	DOB	CDL OR ID CARD NUMBER		
			HOME ADDRSS INCLUDE ZIP CODE		PHONE NUMBER	SEX	RACE

PHOTOGRAPHS

Photos Taken? ☐ YES ☐ NO
☐ Poloraid ☐ 35mm ☐ Other
Number taken: _____
Victim's Injuries: ☐ YES ☐ NO
Suspect's Injuries: ☐ YES ☐ NO
Weapon used: ☐ YES ☐ NO

Photographer: _____

OTHER EVIDENCE

Authorization to Release Medical Records

I authorize release of my medical records which relate to this crime report to the Santa Ana Police Department or the District Attorney's Office for the date(s) _____. The facility and/or staff providing the treatment are released from the responsibility of confidentiality as to those records which relate to diagnosis or treatment on the date(s) shown above. I may withdraw this authorization at any time before the hospital or medical providers have complied and released the information.

PRINT NAME _____   SIGNATURE _____   DATE _____

NARRATIVE

_____

NARRATIVE CONTINUED ☐

Interviews

When interviewing the victim, ask specific questions about what happened (i.e. were you hit with an open hand or a closed fist?). Use descriptive language to describe her emotions and demeanor and try to capture specific words used by the victim. Ask the victim if she feared for her safety: Was she terrified? Did she think she might be killed? And ask about any prior incidents of violence both reported and unreported.

When interviewing the suspect, try to obtain pre-arrest/spontaneous statements. Most people misunderstand when statements are admissible. If a suspect is in custody and being interrogated, he must be read his Miranda rights. If he chooses to waive those rights, the interview can continue. If he is remorseful, find out what happened. What was his involvement or the reasons for his actions? Obtain a post-arrest statement as well. Make sure you have proper advisement and waiver of rights. Lock him into a statement regarding the actual act(s) of violence. Minimize the incident and his actions if necessary to get a suspect to talk and give a truthful and specific statement as to what happened. Do not leave it as a general statement as it will be marginalized in court. Suspects will occasionally begin talking without prompting; this is considered a "spontaneous statement". Listen carefully and document everything!

Finally, anytime it is possible, obtain witness statements. In small communities or apartment buildings, neighbors **always** hear something even if they don't know exactly what happened. Children are also incredibly reliable witnesses as they have not yet learned how to lie skillfully. Special care and attention should be given when interviewing children so they don't feel like they are "telling" on one parent or choosing sides between the two. Oftentimes both the victim and suspect will tell responding officers that the

children were sleeping. It is my experience that children rarely sleep when violence is occurring and if they are, it hasn't been for long. They are valuable sources of information. Ask them if they have ever seen specific acts of violence, who hit who, when, how many times, etc.

Chapter Summary

- There are two types of crimes: misdemeanors and felonies.

- It is common for victims to recant their stories after the incident making a thorough investigation critical for the prosecution of the case.

- How the first responder handles the scene of a misdemeanor will make or break the case.

- Crime scene investigators are able to document the scene in a way that officers and first responders will not be able to do.

- A thorough report, capturing as much information as possible, is critical to the case.

- All injuries should be photographed and documented as to color, size and location.

- Ask specific questions when interviewing a victim.

- Listen for pre-arrest/spontaneous statements when interviewing a suspect.

Chapter Questions

(1) What is the difference between a misdemeanor and a felony?

(2) What are 3 things a first responder can do to help the case at trial?

(3) What 3 components should a good domestic violence report contain?

(4) Why is it important to obtain witness statements? Who may be key witnesses?

Chapter 8: Investigating the Crime Scene

Injury Documentation

Documenting the injuries in a domestic violence case is crucial, especially when it comes time for court.   Veteran officers and crime scene investigators handle their cases as if the victim will be unavailable at the time the case goes to court. They plan for the victim to recant and refuse to cooperate with the district attorney's office since it is such a common occurrence. Failing to describe the injuries creates a "he said, she said" situation, especially since the injury will no longer be visible by the time of the court appearance. The way law enforcement agencies document injuries is to describe the injury in the crime report. A detailed description of an injury such as, "a purplish 4 inch bruise across her left cheek", allows someone to visualize what injuries were present. Including the color and size of the bruise offers a more distinct understanding than if an officer wrote, "a bruise was visible on her cheek." The latter explanation is very vague and will cause people to create a mental picture of what they think a bruise should look like.

Examples of vague injuries vs. descriptive injuries

A cut	A 2" long, ¼" wide bloody laceration
Redness	A red, swollen handprint
Bump	3" diameter purplish-green bump
Scratch	3" long red, swollen, bleeding scratch
Bite mark	2" round, dark red bite mark with precise teeth marks

The best way to document injuries is by photographing them. Some agencies have the officers take photographs, while others utilize their crime scene investigators. Whatever the case, photographs can be used as a way to offer a permanent record of the injuries that were sustained. A police officer should always include the injuries in the crime report, but adding photographs offers better clarification to a jury. When taking photographs of injuries, the photographer should always take a photograph showing the injury with and without a scale or color chart. A scale or color chart helps in determining the size and extent of an injury. Also follow-up photographs should be taken within 24-72 hours of when the initial injury occurred, as the injury could become more pronounced and defined. Bruises are a good example of this. If you've ever bumped your arm and a bruise started to develop, you have probably noticed the bruise change color and become darker a day or two later. This occurs because capillaries under the skin burst after receiving blunt force. The blood from the capillaries settle in the area where the trauma occurred, causing the injury to get darker and more pronounced.

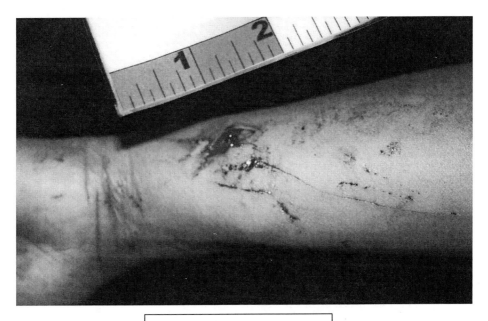

Injury sustained by victim

When talking about documenting injuries, the first thoughts most people have are the victims' injuries. However, it's just as important to document the suspect's injuries as well because some of those injuries could be defensive injuries caused by the victim. Once again, in these situations, a first responder's task is to determine which person was the primary aggressor. Suspects will claim that the victim bit them, showing you a bite mark on their chest. However, if the bite mark on the suspect was a result of the victim trying to get free from being held down, then the bite mark is really a defensive injury. By photographing and documenting this, it can be shown that the victim needed to bite their attacker as a means of self defense. This not only adds credibility to a victim's story, but it could show how desperate the victim was during the attack. It's not always easy determining how injuries were sustained by either party, but the truth of what really occurred may be revealed at a later time. This is why documenting all injuries as soon as possible is so important. It will help prove or disprove one or both party's stories.

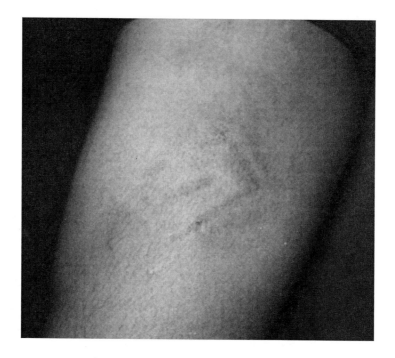

Injury caused by a belt buckle

GROUP ACTIVITY

Break into small groups of 3-4 people. Read the following scenario and respond as if you were a police officer.

You respond to a call at the hospital regarding a victim of domestic violence. You contact the woman, Tanya, and find her curled up in a fetal position in the bed. You see severe facial injuries: bruises, cuts, and swelling. She reluctantly tells you that she woke up this morning at about 1200 hrs after sleeping on the floor of her office in her residence. Her boyfriend came in and accused her of having sex with his friend and said there are pictures of it on the internet. He hit her across her face causing her to fall onto the ground. After she fell, he kicked her several times. He then told her if she wanted to get out, she better do it now because he didn't want to hurt her anymore. At this point, Tanya fled the residence and went to the hospital to use the pay phone to call a taxi. Tanya says she has been living with her boyfriend for 1 ½ years and they have been dating for 4 years. He has been physically abusive throughout the past year. Tanya tells you it is her fault that he had to hit her because she did not have food ready the way he liked it, or didn't answer the phone fast enough. She says he often used a black baton or a taser gun to inflict injuries. Tanya says she doesn't want anything done with this matter and begs you not to look for him. She says her boyfriend's name is D.J. and he is a 27 year old Hispanic man. Because she refuses to give you any further information, you are unable to verify his identity. You respond to the residence and a white male in his late 20's answer the door. When questioned, he tells you Tanya is his executive assistant and their relationship is strictly business. This man, David, says he knew that Tanya has been beat up by her boyfriend, D.J. David only knows D.J. to be a Hispanic in his late 20's. David says he has seen D.J. once or twice, but he probably wouldn't be able to identify him. David says he owns the residence and that Tanya has been living there for the past year because she had no place else to live right now.
(Continued on next page)

While you are talking to David, you see that he is sweating, his T-shirt is soaking wet and he is obviously very nervous. You ask David if he owns a black baton or a taser gun and he reluctantly admits that he does own a baton and he keeps a taser gun in his car for safety reasons. When looking inside the apartment, you observe blood stains on the carpet and walls of the master bedroom.

Questions:
    (1) Identify victim(s) and suspect.
    (2) Identify potential injuries.
    (3) Identify and list crime violations.
    (4) Outline your course of action.

Weapon Collection

Another important aspect of the investigation is the collection and preservation of evidence, particularly if a weapon was used. Since domestic violence is a very volatile crime, many times weapons may be introduced during an attack. Guns and knives are the weapons most people refer to when talking about domestic violence. However, because domestic violence is such a "heat of the moment" type of crime, many of the weapons seen are common household items such as a telephone, TV remote, or even a lamp. If a gun or knife is introduced then there's a good chance that serious injury or even death will result. Of course, this isn't always the case and many of the weapons might even surprise you. I've seen everything from a hair brush to a pot of refried beans used as weapons and the collection and documentation of these weapons is crucial.

Gun documented and collected at a crime scene.

A crime report should state what type of weapon was used during an attack, but taking a photograph of the weapon is the most powerful form of evidence. A beer bottle smashed over a victim's head during a domestic dispute, although serious, may not create too much empathy towards the victim. However, a photograph showing shards of glass from the broken beer bottle scattered all over the kitchen floor with the blood spatter from the victim on the walls, helps someone realize the severity of the attack.

After photographs are taken, the weapon should then be collected. The detectives or district attorney may ask for that weapon to be processed for DNA or fingerprints. Believe it or not, some suspects refuse to admit that a weapon was even used during an attack. If this is the case, the weapon can be processed and we can prove that it was handled by the suspect. Another reason we collect weapons in domestic violence cases is so that the actual weapon can be introduced during court. Even though the jury hears the testimony of the victims and witnesses and review the photographs of the injuries and weapon, bringing the actual weapon into court is very powerful. If a person is attacked with a baseball bat, seeing the bat in court could persuade the "fence sitters" to convict the suspect. Jurors want to see what types of things are used in an attack, so by collecting and preserving weapons, you will allow a jury to view the evidence first hand, which will ultimately assist them in making a decision.

Remember, every state has its own specific laws pertaining to domestic violence and some even require that all weapons be collected by law enforcement personnel when domestic violence occurs. This is to prevent any additional acts of violence and to protect victims in the future. Also, many law enforcement agencies have created specific policies regarding the collection of evidence, so I encourage you to learn your state laws regarding domestic violence and follow your agency's protocols and procedures.

Physical Evidence

Physical evidence can be just about anything. Although most people think documenting the injuries is the most important piece of evidence, there are some items of evidence that are overlooked. In some instances when a victim tells the abuser she is going to call the police, it will enrage the abuser causing him to pull the telephone cord from the wall or even smashing the handset rendering the phone useless.

Cell phone smashed by a suspect

Phone cord ripped out of the wall during an argument

Documenting this can show that the abuser refused to allow the victim to call for help and in some states this is an enhancement to other domestic violence charges. Another powerful piece of evidence is documenting where the children or witnesses, if any, were located and if they saw what occurred. If a husband hits his wife in front of their children, additional charges could be filed, or a determination could be made that the home is unsafe for them. Sometimes alcohol plays a role in a domestic violence case. By documenting the empty cans or bottles, you will corroborate claims that one or both parties were drunk allowing a judge or jury to make a decision utilizing all the facts.

Many officers that respond to domestic violence calls forget to document evidence that is not always obvious. It is very important to thoroughly interview your victim and discover any evidence whether an injury, weapon, or even a statement.

Processing a Domestic Violence Crime Scene

http://www.youtube.com/watch?v=-tNbytC7jYM

CSI Approach to a Child Abuse Scenario

http://www.youtube.com/watch?v=BbkVdpwW2jM

Chapter Summary

- Veteran officers and crime scene investigators handle their cases as if the victim will be unavailable at the time the case goes to court.

- The best way to document injuries is by photographing them.

- It's equally important to document both the victim's and the suspect's injuries.

- Every state has its own specific laws pertaining to domestic violence and some even require that all weapons be collected by law enforcement personnel when domestic violence occurs.

- Physical evidence should be collected whenever possible and officers should pay careful attention to any items that were used as weapons.

Chapter Questions

1) How many ways are there to document injuries and what is the best way?

2) Other than the victim's injuries, who else may have injuries and why is it important to document them?

3) How long after the initial incident should follow-up photographs be taken? Why?

4) Other than firearms, what other items could be considered weapons? Give examples of each and explain how they might be used as a weapon.

5) Give three examples of physical evidence you may find at a crime scene. Explain why documenting this evidence is so important.

Chapter 9: Restraining Orders

There are several types of restraining orders that can be obtained in cases of family violence. They may be called something different depending on the jurisdiction where the crime has occurred, though the similarities make them worth discussing. This chapter will give an overview of each type of order.

Emergency Protective Orders

In most states, Emergency Protective Orders, or EPOs as they are commonly called, can be obtained for family violence, stalking, elder abuse or child abuse cases. They are usually obtained by law enforcement personnel at the scene of the crime if the officer feels that the victim is in imminent danger. The officer will call a judge who will issue an order that is effective immediately. EPOs only last a short time, usually five court days, with the idea that it is enough time for the victim to obtain a more permanent restraining order.

Police and sheriff departments have departmental policies related to serving EPOs. Most departments require their officers to attempt to serve an EPO that has not been served during the same shift. Other departments may require officers to always request an EPO from a judge if an arrest for a domestic violence related crime is made.

An EPO can do several things for the victim. It will require the abuser to stay a certain amount of physical distance from the victim. It will also prevent him from contacting the victim via phone, email, or through a third person. An EPO can protect the victim as well as anyone else living in the home, including the children. It can also protect the victim at work, school, or any other place that she visits on a regular basis.

 http://www.youtube.com/watch?v=i66EnFjl188&list=PL1EF8DC66000EAC5A&feature=plpp

On the following page is one agency's example of an Emergency Protective Order.

(Name): _____ has provided the information in items 1-5.

LAW ENFORCEMENT CASE NUMBER:

1. PERSON(S) TO BE PROTECTED *(insert names of all persons to be protected by this order):*

_____

2. PERSON TO BE RESTRAINED *(name):* _____

Sex: ☐ M ☐ F Ht.: _____ Wt.: _____ Hair color: _____ Eye color: _____ Race: _____ Age: _____ Date of birth: _____

3. The events that cause the protected person to fear immediate and present danger of domestic violence, child abuse, child abduction, elder or dependent adult abuse, or stalking (including workplace violence or civil harassment) are *(give facts and dates; specify weapons):* _____

_____

4. ☐ The person to be protected lives with the person to be restrained and requests an order that the restrained person move out immediately from the address in item 9.

5. a. ☐ The person to be protected has minor children in common with the person to be restrained, and a temporary custody order is requested because of the facts alleged in item 3. A custody order ☐ does ☐ does not exist.

   b. ☐ The person to be protected is a minor child in immediate danger of being abducted by the person to be restrained because of the facts alleged in item 3.

6. ☐ A child welfare worker or probation officer has advised the undersigned that a juvenile court petition
   ☐ will be filed. ☐ will NOT be filed.

7. ☐ Adult Protective Services has been notified.

8. Phone call to *(name of judicial officer):* _____ on *(date):* _____ at *(time):* _____
   ☐ The judicial officer granted the **Emergency Protective Order** that follows.

By: _____

(PRINT NAME OF LAW ENFORCEMENT OFFICER)   (SIGNATURE OF LAW ENFORCEMENT OFFICER)

Agency: _____ Police Department _____ Telephone No.: _____ Badge No.: _____

EMERGENCY PROTECTIVE ORDER

9. To restrained person *(name):* _____

   a. ☐ You must not contact, molest, harass, attack, strike, threaten, sexually assault, batter, telephone, send any messages to, follow, stalk, destroy any personal property, or disturb the peace of each person named in item 1.

   b. ☐ You must ☐ stay away at least _____ yards from each person named in item 1.
      ☐ stay away at least _____ yards from ☐ move out immediately from
      (address): _____

10. ☐ *(Name):* _____ is given temporary care and control of the following minor children of the parties *(names and ages):* _____

11. Reasonable grounds for the issuance of this order exist and an emergency protective order is necessary to prevent the occurrence or recurrence of domestic violence, child abuse, child abduction, elder or dependent adult abuse, or stalking (including workplace violence or civil harassment).

12. **THIS EMERGENCY PROTECTIVE ORDER WILL EXPIRE AT 5:00 P.M. ON:** _____

To protected person: If you need protection for a longer period of time, you must request permanent protective orders at *(court name and address):*

INSERT DATE OF FIFTH COURT DAY OR SEVENTH CALENDAR DAY, WHICHEVER IS EARLIER; DO NOT COUNT DAY THE ORDER IS GRANTED

PROOF OF SERVICE

13. Person served *(name):* _____

14. I personally delivered copies to the person served as follows: Date: _____ Time: _____
    Address: _____

15. At the time of service I was at least 18 years of age and not a party to this cause.

16. My name, address, and telephone number are *(this does not have to be server's home telephone number or address):*

☐ sheriff or marshal

I declare under penalty of perjury under the laws of the State of California that the foregoing is true and correct.

Date: _____

(TYPE OR PRINT NAME OF SERVER)   *(See reverse for important notices)*   (SIGNATURE OF SERVER)

Form Adopted for Mandatory Use
Judicial Council
1295.90 [Rev. January 1, 2000]
Approved by DOJ

EMERGENCY PROTECTIVE ORDER (CLETS)
(Domestic Violence, Child Abuse, Elder or Dependent
Adult Abuse, Workplace Violence, Civil Harassment)
ONE copy to court, ONE copy to restrained person, ONE copy to protected person, ONE copy to issuing agency

152

Civil Restraining Orders

There are two types of civil restraining orders: temporary and permanent. A victim can apply for a temporary restraining order which is usually valid for 30 days. The victim will need some type of "proof" that abuse has occurred or be able to articulate fear for her safety or the safety of her children. A judge will grant the temporary restraining order to allow time to schedule a hearing, and then the judge will decide whether or not a permanent restraining order is necessary. There is no cost to obtain an order of protection.

To obtain a temporary restraining order, the victim will go to the courthouse and complete an application for the order. Many counties have a victim assistance office where advocates are present to help the victim fill out the application and even accompany her to court. The victim will have to fill out a statement describing the type of abuse that has occurred in as specific detail as possible. In most cases, the victim will have to call the abuser from the courthouse to notify him that she is applying for a temporary restraining order and give him the information about the same-day hearing with the judge. After a decision regarding the temporary restraining order, the parties will be given a return date in a few weeks. At this time, the victim will be able to request a permanent restraining order.

After a hearing date has been set, the victim will need to hire a process server or ask someone she knows to serve her partner with the restraining order paperwork and notice of the upcoming hearing. Sometimes a victim will choose to hire a process server because she doesn't know someone who is willing to serve the order; or she doesn't want to put a friend "in the middle" of her and her partner. Having a professional serve the order may also avoid a fight or argument over the order being served. At the hearing, the victim will have to provide proof that abuse or harassment has occurred and that she is in fear for her life.

On the following pages is an example of a civil restraining order: a request for an order followed by the permanent order. The victim fills out an application to present to the judge and once the application is accepted, the judge can issue a permanent order of protection.

Practical Learning Activity

You are victim of family violence and want to get a restraining order against your husband. You don't want to involve the police and think you can handle it on your own.

(1) Research where you would go in your county to file for a Civil Restraining Order.

(2) Get an application and fill it out completely.

(3) Trade applications with someone else in your class and give feedback to each other.

Request for Order

(1) Your name (person asking for protection): _____

Your address *(skip this if you have a lawyer): (If you want your address to be private, give a mailing address instead):*

_____

City: _____ State: _____ Zip: _____

Your telephone number *(optional):* _____

Your lawyer *(if you have one): (Name, address, telephone number, and State Bar number):*

_____

_____

_____

Superior Court of

Case Number:

(2) Name of person you want protection from: _____

Description of that person: Sex: ☐ M ☐ F Height: _____

Weight: _____ Race: _____ Hair Color: _____

Eye Color: _____ Age: _____ Date of Birth: _____

(3) Besides you, who needs protection? *(Family or household members):*

Full Name	Age	Lives with you?	How are they related to you?
_____	_____	☐ Yes ☐ No	_____
_____	_____	☐ Yes ☐ No	_____
_____	_____	☐ Yes ☐ No	_____
_____	_____	☐ Yes ☐ No	_____

(4) What is your relationship to the person in **(2)**? *(Check all that apply):*

a. ☐ We are now married or registered domestic partners.

b. ☐ We used to be married or registered domestic partners.

c. ☐ We live together.

d. ☐ We used to live together.

e. ☐ We are relatives, in-laws, or related by adoption *(specify relationship):* _____

f. ☐ We are dating or used to date.

g. ☐ We are engaged to be married or were engaged to be married.

h. ☐ We are the parents together of a child or children under 18:

Child's Name: _____ Date of Birth: _____

Child's Name: _____ Date of Birth: _____

Child's Name: _____ Date of Birth: _____

☐ *Check here if you need more space.*

i. ☐ We have signed a Voluntary Declaration of Paternity for our child or children. *(Attach a copy if you have one.)*

This is not a Court Order.

(5) Other Court Cases

a. Have you and the person in (2) been involved in another court case? ☐ No ☐ Yes

If yes, where? County: _____ State: _____

What are the case numbers? *(If you know):* _____

What kind of case? *(Check all that apply):*

☐ Registered Domestic Partnership ☐ Divorce/Dissolution ☐ Parentage/Paternity ☐ Legal Separation ☐ Domestic Violence ☐ Criminal ☐ Juvenile ☐ Child Support ☐ Nullity ☐ Civil Harassment ☐ Other *(specify):* _____

b. Are there any domestic violence restraining/protective orders now (criminal, juvenile, family)?

☐ No ☐ Yes *If yes, attach a copy if you have one.*

What orders do you want? Check the boxes that apply to your case. ☑

(6) ☐ Personal Conduct Orders

I ask the court to order the person in (2) not to do the following things to me or any of the people listed in (3):

a. ☐ Harass, attack, strike, threaten, assault (sexually or otherwise), hit, follow, stalk, molest, destroy personal property, disturb the peace, keep under surveillance, or block movements

b. ☐ Contact (either directly or indirectly), or telephone, or send messages or mail or e-mail

The person in (2) will be ordered not to take any action to get the addresses or locations of any protected person, their family members, caretakers, or guardians unless the court finds good cause not to make the order.

(7) ☐ Stay-Away Order

I ask the court to order the person in (2) to stay at least _____ yards away from *(check all that apply):*

a. ☐ Me

b. ☐ The people listed in (3)

c. ☐ My home

d. ☐ My job or workplace

e. ☐ The children's school or child care

f. ☐ My vehicle

g. ☐ Other *(specify):* _____

If the person listed in (2) is ordered to stay away from all the places listed above, will he or she still be able to get to his or her home, school, job, or place of worship? ☐ Yes ☐ No *(If no, explain):* _____

(8) ☐ Move-Out Order

I ask the court to order the person in (2) to move out from and not return to *(address):*

_____

I have the right to live at the above address because *(explain):* _____

(9) ☐ Child Custody, Visitation, and Child Support

I ask the court to order child custody, visitation, and/or child support.

(10) ☐ Spousal Support

You can make this request only if you are married to, or are a registered domestic partner of, the person in (2) and no spousal support order exists.

This is not a Court Order.

What orders do you want? Check the boxes that apply to your case. ☑

(11) ☐ **Record Unlawful Communications**

I ask for the right to record communications made to me by the person in (2) that violate the judge's orders.

(12) ☐ **Property Control**

I ask the court to give *only* me temporary use, possession, and control of the property listed here:

_____

(13) ☐ **Debt Payment**

I ask the court to order the person in (2) to make these payments while the order is in effect:

☐ *Check here if you need more space.*

Pay to: _____ For: _____ Amount: $ _____ Due date: _____

Pay to: _____ For: _____ Amount: $ _____ Due date: _____

Pay to: _____ For: _____ Amount: $ _____ Due date: _____

(14) ☐ **Property Restraint**

I am married to or have a registered domestic partnership with the person in (2). I ask the judge to order that the person in (2) not borrow against, sell, hide, or get rid of or destroy any possessions or property, except in the usual course of business or for necessities of life. I also ask the judge to order the person in (2) to notify me of any new or big expenses and to explain them to the court.

(15) ☐ **Attorney Fees and Costs**

I ask that the person in (2) pay some or all of my attorney fees and costs.

(16) ☐ **Payments for Costs and Services**

I ask that the person in (2) pay the following:

You can ask for lost earnings or your costs for services caused directly by the person in (2) (damaged property, medical care, counseling, temporary housing, etc.). You must bring proof of these expenses to your hearing.

Pay to: _____ For: _____ Amount: $ _____

Pay to: _____ For: _____ Amount: $ _____

Pay to: _____ For: _____ Amount: $ _____

(17) ☐ **Batterer Intervention Program**

I ask the court to order the person listed in (2) to go to a 52-week batterer intervention program and show proof of completion to the court.

(18) **No Fee to Serve (Notify) Restrained Person**

If you want the sheriff or marshal to serve (notify) the restrained person about the orders for free, ask the court clerk what you need to do.

This is not a Court Order.

What orders do you want? Check the boxes that apply to your case. ☑

⑲ ☐ **More Time for Notice**

I need extra time to notify the person in ② about these papers. Because of the facts explained on this form, I want the papers served up to _____ days before the date of the hearing.

If necessary, add additional facts: _____

_____

⑳ ☐ **Other Orders**

What other orders are you asking for? _____

_____

☐ *Check here if you need more space.*

㉑ **Guns or Other Firearms**

I believe the person in ② owns or possesses guns or firearms. ☐ Yes ☐ No ☐ I don't know

If the judge approves the order, the person in ② will be required to sell to a gun dealer or turn in to police any guns or firearms that he or she owns or possesses.

㉒ Describe the most recent abuse.

a. Date of most recent abuse: _____

b. Who was there? _____

c. What did the person in ② do or say that made you afraid?

_____

_____

_____

_____

_____

_____

d. Describe any use or threatened use of guns or other weapons: _____

_____

e. Describe any injuries: _____

_____

f. Did the police come? ☐ No ☐ Yes

If yes, did they give you an Emergency Protective Order? ☐ Yes ☐ No ☐ I don't know

Attach a copy if you have one.

☐ *Check here if you need more space.*

☐ *Check here if the person in ② has abused you (or your children) other times.*

I declare under penalty of perjury under the laws of the State of ⸱ ⸱ ⸱ that the information above is true and correct.

Date: _____

▶

_____ _____

Type or print your name   *Sign your name*

This is not a Court Order.

Case Number:

① Your name: _____

② Name of person you want protection from (restrained person): _____

③ **Describe the 2nd most recent abuse.**

a. Date of 2nd most recent abuse: _____

b. Who was there? _____

c. What did the person in ② do or say to you that made you afraid? _____

_____

_____

_____

_____

_____

_____

_____

_____

_____

_____

_____

_____

_____

_____

d. Describe any use or threatened use of guns or other weapons. _____

_____

_____

_____

e. Describe any injuries. _____

_____

_____

_____

f. Did the police come? ☐ No ☐ Yes

If yes, did they give you an Emergency Protective Order? ☐ Yes ☐ No ☐ I don't know
Attach a copy if you have one.

159

4 **Describe other recent abuse.**

   a. Date of other recent abuse: _____

   b. Who was there? _____

_____

   c. What did the person in ❷ do or say to you that made you afraid? _____

_____

_____

_____

_____

_____

_____

_____

_____

_____

_____

   d. Describe any use or threatened use of guns or other weapons. _____

_____

_____

_____

   e. Describe any injuries. _____

_____

_____

   f. Did the police come? ☐ No   ☐ Yes

      If yes, did they give you an Emergency Protective Order? ☐ Yes   ☐ No   ☐ I don't know
      Attach a copy if you have one.

5 ☐ **Describe other abuse against you or your children.**

_____

_____

_____

_____

_____

Description of Abuse

HOW TO PROCESS A RESTRAINING ORDER

Emergency Protective Order
Used by law enforcement to get an emergency order over nights and weekends

Temporary Restraining Order
* Request for Order
* Description of Abuse
* Temporary Restraining Order and Notice of Hearing

Ex Parte Hearing
Some courts will issue the temporary without an ex-parte hearing.

Temporary Restraining Order and Notice of Hearing
Orders issued by the Judge will be in effect until the Restraining Order Hearing date, any orders crossed out are NOT in effect.

Filing the forms
The Court Clerk will now file the forms and provide the party with 5 certified copies and one extra copy for the Domestic Violence Registry (pursuant to procedures in your court).

Service of the forms
The person requesting the orders must now have copies of all filed forms personally served on the restrained person, as well as a **blank** Answer to Temporary Restraining Order

Proof of Service
Once the forms are served on the restrained person, the Proof of Service must be filled out by the person who served the restrained person and filed with the Court.

Answer from Restrained Person
The person to be restrained may file the answer and serve the person requesting the order. This should be done prior to the hearing

Restraining Order Hearing
The party must attend this hearing, even if the person to be restrained has not yet been served. The court will continue the hearing and re-issue the temporary orders to allow time for service. If the restrained person has been served the Court can issue the restraining order or set a contested hearing.

Contested Hearing
The party must attend this hearing for the Judge to issue a restraining order. At this hearing each party may bring evidence and witnesses. The court can either dismiss the case or grant the request for restraining order.

Judge Issues the Restraining Order
The Court Clerk will file the order, provide the party with 5 certified copies and make one extra copy to be forwarded to the Domestic Violence Registry (pursuant to procedures in your court).

Serve the Restraining Order After Hearing
The restraining order must be personally served on the restrained person if they were not present at the hearing and the orders differ from the original order and notice of hearing. If the orders do not differ from the initial request the restaining order can be served by mail on the restrained person.

Proof of Service
Must be filed with the Court after service on the restrained person.

161

Temporary Restraining Order and Notice of Hearing

(1) Name of person asking for protection (protected person):

_____

Protected person's address *(skip this if you have a lawyer)*: *(If you want your address to be private, give a mailing address instead)*:

_____

City: _____ State: _____ Zip: _____
Telephone number: _____
Protected person's lawyer *(if any)*: *(Name, address, telephone number, and State Bar number)*:

_____
_____
_____

Fill in court name and street address:

Superior Court

(2) Restrained person's name:

_____

Description of that person: Sex: ☐ M ☐ F Height: _____
Weight: _____ Race: _____ Hair Color: _____
Eye Color: _____ Age: _____ Date of Birth: _____

Fill in case number:

Case Number:

(3) List the full names of all family or household members protected by this order: _____

(4) Court Hearing Date
Clerk will fill out section below.

Hearing Date → Date: _____ Time: _____ Name and address of court if different from above: _____

Dept.: _____ Rm.: _____ _____

To the person in **(2)**: At the hearing, the judge can make restraining orders that last for up to 5 years. The judge can also make other orders about your children, child support, spousal support, money, and property. File an answer on Form DV-120 before the hearing. At the hearing, you can tell the judge that you do not want the orders against you. Even if you do not attend the hearing, you *must* obey the orders.

To the person in **(1)**: At the hearing, the judge will consider whether denial of any orders will jeopardize your safety and the safety of children for whom you are requesting custody, visitation, and child support. Safety concerns related to the financial needs of you and your children will also be considered.

(5) Temporary Orders (Ordenes Temporales)
Any orders made in this form end at the time of the court hearing in **(4)**, unless a judge extends them.
Read this form carefully. All checked boxes ☑ and items 10 and 11 are court orders.

This is a Court Order.

(6) ☐ **Personal Conduct Orders**

The person in ② must *not* do the following things to the protected people listed in ① and ③:

a. ☐ Harass, attack, strike, threaten, assault (sexually or otherwise), hit, follow, stalk, molest, destroy personal property, disturb the peace, keep under surveillance, or block movements

b. ☐ Contact (either directly or indirectly), or telephone, or send messages or mail or e-mail
   ☐ Except for brief and peaceful contact as required for court-ordered visitation of children unless a criminal protective order says otherwise

c. ☐ Take any action, directly or through others, to get the addresses or locations of any protected persons or of their family members, caretakers, or guardians. *(If item c is not checked, the court has found good cause not to make this order.)*

Peaceful written contact through a lawyer or through a process server or another person in order to serve legal papers is allowed and does not violate this order.

☐ A criminal protective order on Form CR-160 is in effect. Case Number: _____
County *(if known):* _____ Expiration Date: _____ *(If more orders, list them in item* ⑯*)*

(7) ☐ **Stay-Away Order**

The person in ② must stay at least_____ yards away from:

a. ☐ The person listed in ①   d. ☐ The children's school or child care
b. ☐ The people listed in ③   e. ☐ Other *(specify):* _____
c. ☐ Home ☐ Job ☐ Vehicle of person in ①

(8) ☐ **Move-Out Order**

The person in ② must take only personal clothing and belongings needed until the hearing and move out immediately from *(address):* _____

(9) ☐ **Child Custody and Visitation Order**

a. ☐ You and the other parent must make an appointment for court mediation *(address and phone number):* _____

(10) **No Guns or Other Firearms or Ammunition**

The person in ② cannot own, possess, have, buy or try to buy, receive or try to receive, or in any other way get guns, firearms, or ammunition.

(11) **Turn in or sell guns or firearms.**

The person in ②:

• Must sell to a licensed gun dealer or turn in to police any guns or firearms that he or she has or controls. This must be done within 24 hours of being served with this order.

• Must bring a receipt to the court within 48 hours of being served with this order, to prove that guns and firearms have been turned in or sold.

(12) ☐ **Property Control**

Until the hearing, *only* the person in ① can use, control, and possess the following property and things:

_____

_____

This is a Court Order.

Your name: _____

(13) ☐ **Property Restraint**

If the people in ① and ② are married to each other or are registered domestic partners, they must not transfer, borrow against, sell, hide, or get rid of or destroy any property, except in the usual course of business or for necessities of life. In addition, each person must notify the other of any new or big expenses and explain them to the court. *(The person in ② cannot contact the person in ① if the court has made a "no contact" order.)*

(14) ☐ **Unlawful communications may be recorded.**

The person in ① can record communications made by the person in ② that violate the judge's orders.

(15) **No Fee to Notify (Serve) Restrained Person**

If the sheriff serves this order, he or she will do it for free.

(16) ☐ **Other Orders** *(specify):* _____

_____

_____

(17) If the judge makes a restraining order at the hearing, which has the same orders as in this form, the person in ② will get a copy of that order by mail at his or her last known address. *(Write restrained person's address here):*

_____

If this address is not correct, or to know if the orders were made permanent, contact the court.

(18) ☐ **Time for Service**

Ⓐ **To: Person Asking for Order**	**Ⓑ** **To: Person Served With Order**
Someone 18 or over—**not you or the other protected people**—must personally "serve" a copy of this order to the restrained person at least _____ days before the hearing.	If you want to respond in writing, someone 18 or over—**not you**—must "serve" Form DV-120 on the person in ①, then file it with the court at least _____ days before the hearing.

Date: _____   ▶ _____

Judge (or Judicial Officer)

Certificate of Compliance With VAWA

This temporary protective order meets all Full Faith and Credit requirements of the Violence Against Women Act, 18 U.S.C. § 2265 (1994) (VAWA) upon notice of the restrained person. This court has jurisdiction over the parties and the subject matter; the restrained person has been or will be afforded notice and a timely opportunity to be heard as provided by the laws of this jurisdiction. **This order is valid and entitled to enforcement in each jurisdiction throughout the 50 United States, the District of Columbia, all tribal lands, and all U.S. territories, commonwealths, and possessions and shall be enforced as if it were an order of that jurisdiction.**

This is a Court Order.

Temporary Restraining Order
and Notice of Hearing (CLETS—TRO)

Your name: _____

Warnings and Notices to the Restrained Person in ❷

⑲ If you do not obey this order, you can be arrested and charged with a crime.

- It is a felony to take or hide a child in violation of this order. You can go to prison and/or pay a fine.
- If you travel to another state or to tribal lands or make the protected person do so, with the intention of disobeying this order, you can be charged with a federal crime.
- If you do not obey this order, you can go to prison and/or pay a fine.

⑳ You cannot have guns, firearms, and/or ammunition.

You cannot own, have, possess, buy or try to buy, receive or try to receive, or otherwise get guns, firearms, and/or ammunition while the order is in effect. If you do, you can go to jail and pay a $1,000 fine. You must sell to a gun dealer or turn in to police any guns or firearms that you have or control. The judge will ask you for proof that you did so. If you do not obey this order, you can be charged with a crime. Federal law says you cannot have guns or ammunition if you are subject to a restraining order made after a noticed hearing.

㉑ After You Have Been Served With a Restraining Order

- Obey all the orders.
- If you want to respond, fill out Form DV-120. Take it to the court clerk with the forms listed in item ㉒.
- File DV-120 and have all papers served on the protected person by the date listed in item ⑱ of this form.
- At the hearing, tell the judge if you agree or disagree with the orders requested.
- Even if you do not attend the hearing, the judge can make the restraining orders last for 5 years.

㉒ Child Custody, Visitation, and Support

- Child Custody and Visitation: If you do not go to the hearing, the judge can make custody and visitation orders for your children without hearing your side.
- Child Support: The judge can order child support based on the income of both parents. The judge can also have that support taken directly from your paycheck. Child support can be a lot of money, and usually you have to pay until the child is 18. File and serve a *Financial Statement* (Form FL-155) or an *Income and Expense Declaration* (Form FL-150) so the judge will have information about your finances. Otherwise, the court may make support orders without hearing your side.
- Spousal Support: File and serve a *Financial Statement* (Form FL-155) or an *Income and Expense Declaration* (Form FL-150) so the judge will have information about your finances. Otherwise, the court may make support orders without hearing your side.

㉓ **Requests for Accommodations**
Assistive listening systems, computer-assisted real-time captioning, or sign language interpreter services are available if you ask at least five days before the proceeding.

This is a Court Order.

**Temporary Restraining Order
and Notice of Hearing (CLETS—TRO)**

Instructions for Law Enforcement

(24) **Start Date and End Date of Orders**

The start date is the date next to the judge's signature on page 3. The orders end on the hearing date on page 1 or the hearing date on Form DV-125, if attached.

(25) **Arrest Required If Order Is Violated**

If an officer has probable cause to believe that the restrained person had notice of the order and has disobeyed the order, the officer must arrest the restrained person.

(26) **Notice/Proof of Service**

Law enforcement must first determine if the restrained person had notice of the orders. If notice cannot be verified, the restrained person must be advised of the terms of the orders. If the restrained person then fails to obey the orders, the officer must enforce them.

Consider the restrained person "served" (noticed) if:

- The officer sees a copy of the *Proof of Service* or confirms that the *Proof of Service* is on file; *or*
- The restrained person was at the restraining order hearing or was informed of the order by an officer.

(27) **If the Protected Person Contacts the Restrained Person**

Even if the protected person invites or consents to contact with the restrained person, the orders remain in effect and must be enforced. The protected person cannot be arrested for inviting or consenting to contact with the restrained person. The orders can be changed only by another court order.

(28) **Child Custody and Visitation**

- Custody and visitation orders are on Form DV-140, items (3) and (4). They are sometimes also written on additional pages or referenced in DV-140 or other orders that are not part of the restraining order.

Clerk's Certificate

[seal]

I certify that this Temporary Restraining Order is a true and correct copy of the original on file in the court.

Date: _____ Clerk, by _____ , Deputy

This is a Court Order.

Temporary Restraining Order
and Notice of Hearing (CLETS—TRO)

Criminal Protective Orders

Criminal Protective Orders are issued in some states by the courts if someone is charged with a family violence crime. The court's intent is to protect the victim from further abuse and to do so without her having to go through the arduous process of getting a civil restraining order. In most situations, criminal protective orders will remain valid throughout the duration of the court case. Similar to other protective orders, they prevent the victim and her abuser from having any type of contact, keep him from returning to the house, and also will protect any children.

On the following page is an example of a Superior Court's Criminal Protective Order.

SUPERIOR COURT

PEOPLE OF THE STATE OF

PLAINTIFF,

VS.

DEFENDANT.

CASE NUMBER

☐   **D.V. PROTECTIVE ORDER (Probation)** - Mandatory
☐   **CRIMINAL COURT PROTECTIVE ORDER**
☐   **CRIMINAL COURT PROTECTIVE ORDER** - Prison Sentence (Order as part of plea agreement)
☐   **TERMINATION/MODIFICATION OF PRIOR ORDER**

THE COURT HEREBY ORDERS:

1. (NAME OF RESTRAINED PERSON)_____

DESCRIPTION: DOB: DL: TATTOOS/SCARS:

RACE: HAIR: EYES: HT: WT:

   ☐ a. Shall not stalk, sexually abuse, harass, threaten, or commit any violence upon the protected person(s) named below.
   ☐ b. Shall have no contact with protected person(s) directly, indirectly or through a third party except by an attorney of record.
   ☐ c. Shall not come within ___ yards of the person(s) named below, their home, work or children's school.
      DO NOT GO TO THESE PLACES: _____

2. NAMES OF PROTECTED PERSON(S):_____

3. The protected persons may not allow you to violate this order. **DO NOT** respond to requests from the protected person to visit or return phone calls.

4. A copy of the D.V. Protective Order is available to law enforcement

5. Persons subject to a D.V. Protective Order are prohibited from owning, using or possessing firearms.

6. Other orders: _____

7. ☐ a. The restrained person is present in court and informed of this order. No further proof of service is needed.
   ☐ b. The restrained person is not present in court and shall be personally served with a copy of this order.
      (Proof of Service is attached or has been placed in court file)

8. This order remains in effect until:
   ☐ a. Date and time shown. Date: _____ Time: _____
   ☐ b. Termination of probation on _____

9. This restrained person shall not attempt to , nor threaten, harass or dissuade any victim or witness connected to this case from reporting a crime, attending court, or testifying in any court hearing.

10. ☐ The Protective Order previously made in this case against the restrained person named in item 1 is terminated
    ☐ The Protective Order previously made in this case is modified as follows: _____
    _____

Date:

_____
JUDGE OF THE SUPERIOR COURT

VIOLATION OF THIS COURT ORDER MAY BE A NEW CRIME, A PROBATION OR PAROLE VIOLATION OR A VIOLATION OF THE TERMS OF YOUR RELEASE FROM CUSTODY AND/OR BAIL.

White - Court; **Green** - Defendant; **Canary** - D.A.; **Pink** - Protected Person(s); **Gold** - Law Enforcement

(USE BALL POINT PEN-PRESS HARD)

How Restraining Orders Help

Once a restraining order has been issued, the victim should carry a copy of the order with her wherever she goes. She should also make sure that her workplace, her children's school, and any other place that she and her children frequent have a copy of the order. If the abuser contacts her or attempts to contact her, he is breaking the law and the police should be called immediately.

Restraining orders require the abuser to stay away from the victim. Usually, it states he must stay a minimum of 100 yards away from the victim. The abuser can be arrested if he is found to be in violation of the order. While it isn't a guarantee of protection (the abuser can choose to ignore the order and contact the victim anyway), in a majority of cases it serves as a deterrent to the abuser. It also affords another tool for the victim to use in future situations because once he has violated a restraining order, he has broken the law and can be held accountable.

http://www.youtube.com/watch?v=1w9ppTvypWw

Problems / Questions That Arise

The protected party should make sure that her local police department has a copy of the protective order on file. It is also important to know that restraining orders are valid across state lines – you just have to look for the party names and both the court certified stamp and the expiration date. In many states, any person subject to a restraining order is prohibited from obtaining, purchasing or attempting to purchase a firearm.

Chapter Summary

- Emergency Protective Orders are usually obtained by law enforcement personnel at the scene of the crime if the officer feels that the victim is in imminent danger.

- There are two types of civil restraining orders: temporary and permanent.
  - Temporary orders are granted for 30 days to allow time to schedule a hearing.
  - Permanent orders are granted for 3-10 years.

- Criminal Protective Orders are issued in some states by the courts if someone is charged with a family violence crime.

- Restraining orders require the abuser to stay away from his victim and he can be arrested if he is found to be in violation of the order.

Chapter Questions

(1) What is an EPO and who can issue one?

(2) What are the differences between a Criminal Protective Order and a Civil Restraining Order?

(3) How does someone obtain a Temporary Restraining Order? Who can apply for one?

Chapter 10: Resources

Family Violence Advocates

Through VAWA funding, many police agencies and district attorney offices around the country provide advocates for victims of violent crimes, and more specifically, victims of family violence. Advocates are available to provide information and resources to victims, accompany them to court, explain the case status, assist them with getting a restraining order, and provide immediate crisis intervention. Many police agencies have found it to be advantageous to employ advocates so there is a dedicated person on-scene to provide emotional support and work directly with the victim, thus leaving officers available to investigate the case.

As a family violence advocate, I worked for several years directly out of the District Attorney's office on felony cases of domestic violence, child abuse, elder abuse and sexual assault. I was available to:

- sit with the victim during the court case and explain things to her along the way
- help her navigate the confusing court system
- provide her with resources such as counseling or even a shelter

- work with the District Attorney's investigators to advocate for the victim's rights
- and sometimes I was just a friendly face during a turbulent time

When I worked in the Investigation Unit of a large municipal law enforcement agency, part of my job was to ride along with officers as a first responder. As a team, we responded to any calls for service for family violence. I helped victims find an emergency shelter, provided crisis intervention, helped calm screaming children and anything else that needed to be done to get the victim to a safe and secure place. I also provided follow-up on the victim's case after her abuser was arrested. I went to court with her and walked with her through the entire legal proceedings against her partner.

For many victims, having someone to walk beside them was all they needed to follow through with leaving the abuser or getting a restraining order. Their lives were in such chaos, they could not figure out the next step to take or where to even start. Either they did not have friends and family close by or their inner circle was so tired of trying to convince her to leave the situation they had given up long ago. Also, the court system can be very confusing to navigate; especially to someone who is in crisis or someone who doesn't speak English. I got them the help they needed even if it was just someone to meet at the courthouse to sit with them and explain everything that was happening.

Family Violence Emergency Response Teams (FVERTs)

A FVERT is staffed by specially trained police officers who are paired with specially trained volunteer victim advocates. The team generally works the evening shift, (Fridays and Saturdays, 6 p.m. – 2 a.m. and Sundays, 6 p.m. – 12 a.m.) responding to any family violence calls for service. These are typically the hours that have the highest percentage of calls reporting family violence. The officer never had to be the "handling" officer so he would be available for any domestic violence calls for service. Their sole purpose was to be available to respond to calls for service to provide crisis intervention to the victim and her children. Oftentimes it included giving resource information or even transporting the victim to a shelter. The program is invaluable for everyone involved. The officers who "handle" the call understand that advocates are there to work closely with the victim and help decipher what actually occurred. They also know advocates will deal with the volatile emotions that are almost always present during these types of calls.

Batterer's Intervention Programs

Batterer Intervention Programs (BIPs) are designed for men who have been arrested for domestic violence or men who would be arrested if their actions were reported to the police. The programs usually consist of a variety of educational classes and treatment groups, sometimes offering individual counseling and case management. The purpose of BIPs is multifaceted: enhance victim safety, provide accountability and justice for batterers, and ultimately rehabilitation.

Batterers are charged for the programs (although most programs offer a sliding scale fee) and must arrive on-time each week for the duration of the program, without missing a class. Programs vary in length but are typically 26 or 52 weeks. Often if the abuser had been drinking when he was arrested, he will be ordered to attend a substance abuse component of the batterer's intervention program as well.

According to a 2006 report in California, only about half of men who enter a BIP actually fulfill the program requirement ("Batterer Intervention Programs", California State Auditors, Bureau of State Audits, 2006). Unfortunately, not all programs report violations to the courts as they are instructed to do. Additionally, some courts that are notified simply send batterers back to the program without imposing any additional fees or jail time. This lack of accountability for the batterers significantly reduces the effectiveness of the programs. Program effectiveness is also impacted by a lack of strict monitoring of the BIPs by state officials. If the judge, who receives monthly progress reports from the program facilitators, believes the batterer would benefit from more time in the program, it is within his right to order him to additional weeks in the program. Also, if the batterer misses a session or arrives late, he may be ordered to attend additional sessions.

I have seen these programs be very effective for families. If the batterer is willing to take ownership for his actions and seeks help, the entire family is impacted. By attending a BIP, the batterer will learn what his triggers are, how to deal with them, and how to handle conflict with his wife or girlfriend in a healthy way. For men who are committed to change, it is not uncommon for them to attend an entire 52-week program without missing a single class. One of the amazing things about BIPs is how the "veteran" attendees become mentors and coaches for the "newbies". Because the program operates every week of the year, you can find men graduating the same day a new man is starting.

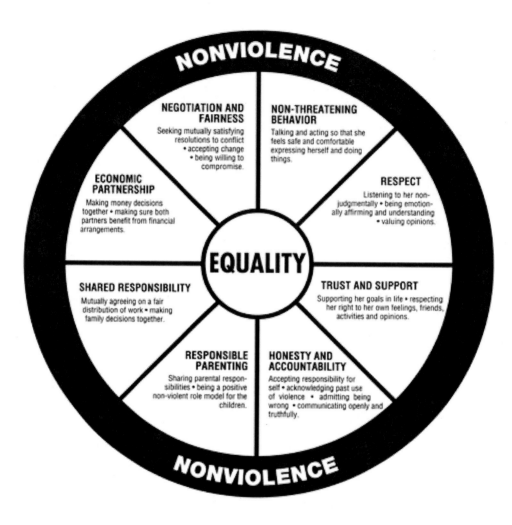

Relationship Equality Wheel

Developed by D.A.R.T. / Palm Beach Gardens, Florida

Family Violence Prevention Fund

The Family Violence Prevention Fund's mission is to work "to prevent violence within the home, and in the community, to help those whose lives are devastated by violence because everyone has the right to live free of violence." (www.endabuse.org) For the past 20+ years, the FVPF has worked to end violence against women and children. They were instrumental in passing the VAWA in 1994, detailed in chapter 4, and continue to provide valuable research on this subject. They have also helped transform the way health care providers, law enforcement agencies, judges and others address family violence. Visit their website for comprehensive information on public policy, facts about family violence and sexual assault, and ways to get involved.

National Domestic Violence Hotline: 1.800.799.SAFE (7233)

This hotline is operated 24 hours a day, 365 days a year by advocates who are available to talk, provide crisis intervention, create a safety plan or give information and referrals. It is available to victims or anyone calling on their behalf in all 50 states, Puerto Rico and the U.S. Virgin Islands. With assistance in English and Spanish, and access to an interpreter service with more than 170 languages, it is the most comprehensive hotline available for abuse victims. (www.ndvh.org)

"But I Love Him" by Dr. Jill Murray

Dr. Murray is the leading international expert on teen dating violence. In addition to speaking to thousands of high school students every year, she has appeared on Oprah, Good Morning America Weekend Edition and 20/20. In this groundbreaking book, Dr. Murray takes a holistic look at the issue addressing everything from defining this type of abuse to specific ways to address it with someone you love. Her stories and intimate knowledge of the subject matter provide incredible insight. (www.drjillmurray.com)

National Teen Dating Abuse Helpline: 1.866.331.9474

This is a national 24-hour resource for teens and their loved ones. It can be accessed via the phone number listed above or by visiting www.loveisrespect.org. Definitions of abuse, fast facts, and resources (including a Teen Dating Bill of Rights) can easily be accessed.

RAINN (Rape, Abuse and Incest National Network)

This is the nation's largest anti-sexual assault organization. RAINN's prevention and education efforts include working with the entertainment industry, media, colleges and local communities to help raise awareness about issues related to sexual assault. In addition, RAINN provides support to sexual assault victims through two hotlines as well as through their website, www.rainn.org.

Conclusion

While working alongside family violence victims, I have heard hundreds of stories of abuse. And to me they weren't just stories – there are names and faces behind each one. They involve real people who are living with this painful and terrifying secret each and every day. And while there are some women who for a variety of reasons are not able to walk away from a violent relationship, there are thousands of courageous women who are doing just that. It is for all of these survivors that I wrote this book!

Family violence should not be a private matter that is handled behind closed doors. It is a national health issue and something all of us should be concerned about. Statistics show that it is our neighbor, our friend or our family member that is being abused – and we don't even know it! I hope after reading this book you understand family violence a little better and the next time you suspect someone is being abused, rather than casting judgment, dismissing the possibility that it is happening or simply doing nothing, you will offer your help, encouragement and support. If we as a society take action, family violence could be eradicated, or at least significantly reduced. It may seem like a daunting task, but it is achievable if we are willing to take the necessary steps. Thank you for your willingness to take the first step by reading this book, but don't let it stop here. Seek out your next step, and the next and the next one after that until family violence is a thing of the past.

Glossary of Common Terms

Advocate -- an individual who works with victims and survivors of domestic and sexual violence, providing confidential, emotional support and assistance with legal, social service and medical issues.

Arraignment -- procedure when the accused is brought before the court to plead to a criminal charge.

Common-Law Marriage -- a relationship in which a couple lives together as though they are married, without having gone through a legal ceremony.

Compensation -- financial reimbursement for any damages and suffering that a victim may have received as a result of abuse.

Contempt -- when a court order is willfully and knowingly violated.

Crisis Center -- a program established to provide free 24-hour confidential, emergency support and assistance, 7 days a week, to victims of domestic violence and sexual assault, regardless of age, race, gender, sexual orientation, economic status, physical or mental ability, and political or philosophical beliefs.

Defendant -- the person who is accused of a crime.

Disposition -- final settlement or sentencing of a criminal case.

Discovery -- process by which a party is granted the right, by the court, to have access to information needed for a court case, including access to income and assets information in divorces and other support cases.

Domestic Violence Protective Order -- an order, placed by the courts, available to someone who has been subject to actual or threatened physical violence by a family or household member, or a current or former intimate or sexual partner.

Emergency Protective Order -- a protective order that can be obtained when the courts are closed

Equality Wheel -- an illustration of the concepts of equality and non-violent behaviors and interactions in a relationship.

Ex Parte -- a party can request emergency assistance of the courts under circumstances where it is not possible or advisable to notify the other party before the court considers the request

Felony -- a criminal offense punishable by more than one year in jail and/or a monetary fine of more than $1000.

Hung Jury -- a jury unable to make a unanimous decision in a trial.

Indictment -- a formal charge against the defendant.

Jurisdiction -- the cities or towns over which a court has power to hear cases.

Lawyer Referral Service -- a legal service which provides legal information and referrals to attorneys statewide.

Mediation -- a non-adversarial process in which a neutral third party acts to encourage and help disputing parties reach a mutually acceptable agreement. May not be a good option when domestic violence is present.

Misdemeanor -- a criminal offense punishable by a monetary fine, and/or a jail sentence of one year or less.

Plaintiff -- a person who begins a court action.

Plea Bargaining -- the process where the accused in a case and the prosecuting attorney work out a mutually satisfactory agreement, which then goes before the court for approval.

Power and Control Wheel -- a wheel diagram which describes aspects of abusive behaviors related to power and control issues.

Pro Bono -- free legal representation.

Pro Se -- representing oneself in a court action or procedure.

Probable Cause Hearing – (also known as a Preliminary Hearing) a hearing in which it is determined as to whether or not there is enough evidence to go forth with a criminal trial.

Protective Order -- see Domestic Violence Protective Order.

Rape Drug -- a drug, such as GHB or Rohypnol, which is used to render someone helpless or unconscious for the purpose of committing a sexual assault.

Sentencing Hearing -- a hearing to reveal the sentence of the accused in a criminal case.

Sexual Assault -- formerly known as "rape," sexual penetration, however slight, with someone against his or her will or without consent.

Sexual Assault Medical Exam -- a physical, gynecological exam performed to make sure the victim of a sexual assault is not physically hurt, and to collect evidence of a sexual assault.

Statute of Limitations -- a declaration that no case will be brought forward after a certain amount of time (statutes vary depending on the type of crime).

Stipulation -- a legal agreement.

Telephonic Order -- an emergency protective order received at a police station, approved by a judge over the telephone.

Temporary Court Order -- a court order which is to last for a set, limited amount of time.

Temporary Protective Order -- a protective order which lasts for up to 30 days, or until the final hearing.

Victim/Witness Advocate -- advocates available through the prosecutor's office to assist victims with criminal processes.